Jesus Has
Left the Building

Jesus Has
Left the Building

Peter Keese

Foreword by Ward B. Ewing

WIPF & STOCK · Eugene, Oregon

JESUS HAS LEFT THE BUILDING

Wipf & Stock
An Imprint of Wipf and Stock Publishers
199 W. 8th Ave., Suite 3
Eugene, OR 97401

www.wipfandstock.com

ISBN 13: 978-1-62564-973-7

Manufactured in the U.S.A.

To Helen, my life's companion who has traveled with me through thick and thin and whose constancy and good humor sustain me; and to our children, William and Kate, and their children, all of who continue to delight and enlighten me. My siblings and their offspring and my in-laws and their spouses and offspring all have enriched my life and life experiences, as well. Though they are not "blood" kin, Helen's younger brother, Allston, his wife, Dana, and their three children, are surely part of our immediate family. I am very fortunate to be in such a loving and supportive family, and I am grateful to them all. This book may explain some of my thinking to them, but, more importantly, even if they disagree, it may encourage them, as they have me, to think independently and to rejoice in all the rich "colors" of life fully lived.

"Tell all the truth, but tell it slant."

EMILY DICKINSON

Contents

Foreword

FOLLOWING THE DEFEAT OF Licinius in 323, Constantine became the sole ruler of the Roman world. Now there was one emperor, one law, one citizenship for all free men. To Constantine's essentially political mind, to complete the process of unification, there must be one religion, the Christianity he had already embraced, legalized, and officially supported. Unfortunately, from the Emperor's perspective, the theological divisions in the church threatened this unity. To resolve the divisions, in 325 he called the first general council of the church in Nicaea.

The establishment of Christianity as the official, privileged, state-supported religion is seen by many today as destructive to the spirituality of the early church which depended on commitment, sometimes even in the face of persecution, rather than conformity. The established church prospered, the position of the clergy was enhanced, and the institution became—for good or for ill—a major player in social and political issues. Today this position of privilege is declining, and many rejoice as the church must become more and more dependent on the committed.

One area of religious life deeply affected by the establishment of Christianity was the assumption that theological conformity is essential to unity. Theological agreement was certainly not characteristic of the church in its first three hundred years; it has not been achievable since 1517 and the Reformation. What the church held in common (and what identified the church as Christian) was the story of Jesus, the resurrection, and the record of the spread of the early church; interpretation of the story varied. The push for theological uniformity in the church came not from the church but from the emperor Constantine. When Jesus prayed at the Last Supper for the unity of his followers (John 17), he speaks of relationships, of knowing and loving one another. He spoke of a new commandment—that we love one another as he loved (John 15)—and he gave an example by washing the disciples' feet (John 13). Constantine, on the other hand, sought theological unity to serve his political agenda. One must ask how important agreement is to loving.

The changes the church is presently undergoing are dramatic, and much has been written regarding the structural and social transformation that is occurring. Within this context of change, Peter Keese communicates his own thoughts, stories, insights, and wisdom that come from over fifty years as a priest in the Episcopal Church. He is not particularly concerned about church organization and structure. He seems unconcerned about membership decline or loss of prestige. Rather he shares freeing insights that renew our theology, our understanding of the church as community, and the joy of discovering God's incarnate action. His thoughts are affirmative reflections based on a life of experience in the church without concern about whether or not the post-Christendom church is positive or negative. We are in a new age and new thinking is required.

There is a natural tendency within religion to desire to "know the truth" and to impose it on others. Since religion is a fundamental foundation for life, knowing that "the truth" is true seems self-evidently important. However, if "the truth" is true, then the evidence should be convincing, so why the need to have others agree to our perception of truth, why the need to persecute those who differ? When does the alliance between the anxiety of human beings and the control needs of an institution become detrimental to relationships formed by servant loving?

Religion has a tendency to want a clear demarcation of who is in and who is out. When does this need for clarity about the community come from loving service and when from fear and the institutional need to control? Perhaps the institutional needs of religion would have led the church to articulate "the truth," impose it on others, and use it to mark clearly who is in and who is out; however, historically this assumption that agreement leads to unity comes from a Roman Emperor.

In this very readable volume, Peter invites us to stretch our hearts and minds in this time of change. Writing out of a deep love for the life we receive as a gift of grace, he invites us to let go of the anxiety and fears surrounding the loss of membership and the decline in the prestige and privilege of the institutional church and consider what new thing God may be doing. He invites us to take off the blinders imposed by traditional teaching and consider more fully the understanding and impact of "incarnation," bible stories, community, sin, salvation, saviors, and good news.

Too often traditional teaching has been formed by the institutional church's needs for certainty and control instead of by the rich and multifaceted insights into the ways of God. One can only wonder if part of the reason for the movement of people away from organized religion lies in an understanding of God that has been reduced to meet human needs rather than an understanding large enough to include all creation—earth's deserts and seas, the sun, the moon, the stars and the galaxies

From 1985 to 1998 I served as the Rector of Trinity Church in downtown Buffalo. Tom Heath, who had served as Rector some fifteen years previous, had a metaphor he used to describe his understanding about God—a metaphor that several parishioners shared with me which reflects how powerful this metaphor was for them.

Tom had a summer cabin on Cape Cod. He shared about his cabin, "I know the Cape where my cabin is located. I know the tidal pools where I can find specimens at low tide. I know how the weather can roll in, when a nor'easter is approaching. I know the best time of day to fish and the changes each season brings. I know where I can swim and where the bottom is too rough or the waves too dangerous. But I cannot say that I know the Atlantic

Ocean or all the oceans in the world. My knowledge ends a few hundred yards from my cabin.

And he continued, "Such is my knowledge of God. I know something of God from my experience, but to say I have full or complete knowledge about God is as foolish as saying I know the oceans of the world because of my experience on Cape Cod."

This metaphor reflects the beginning premise in all theology. God is beyond our knowing, even beyond the ability of language to describe. Thus all knowledge of God is at best partial, and all language about God is metaphorical. Any concept we have of God is like saying we know about the ocean because we know a cove off Cape Cod. Our concepts are too small. Those of us who accept this premise begin talking about God humbly, use "I-statements," and speak primarily from our personal experience.

Peter uses his personal experience to reflect on the traditional theological categories like God, incarnation, sin, salvation, messiah, and church. In the process of personal reflection, he encourages the reader to be open to amplifying such concepts beyond what he or she may have learned as a child. The failure of many churches to provide quality education for adults has left many with simplistic understandings of religion that fail to apply in a scientific world view, fail to touch the heart, or fail to motivate for action.

Even the use of words represents a difficulty in talking about God. Words describe concepts and communicate with the mind. But faith is not primarily about the mind, about what one thinks. Rather faith comes when the heart is touched, when we have been affected emotionally. Theology, doctrine, and intellectual arguments do not touch us emotionally; we are touched emotionally through actions and stories. Religion too often seeks to communicate about God by the use of the intellect through theology and dogma. Faith, spirituality, is communicated by sharing stories. The power of story lies in its ability to intrigue and hook us. We are engaged, gaining one insight now from the story and then at another time another insight. A story is not limited to a specific event or question, but it engages the hearer and provides insights into a multitude of situations. Peter's use of story helps to move us beyond intellectual belief to a spirituality of loving service.

Over the past thirty-five years I have been involved with Alcoholics Anonymous. Central in that program of recovery is the sharing of stories. Talking about alcoholism or about the need to stop drinking with someone who suffers from this disease is talking to a person's intellect; it does not bring change. But hearing the personal story of a recovering alcoholic and identifying with the speaker—"that sounds just like me"—and seeing that the story teller is sober, joyous, and free, gives the still suffering alcoholic hope—hope that invites the person into the community where recovery can be found. Information instructs the mind; change comes when stories touch the heart. Stories not only connect with the emotions, renew the mind, and heal relationships, they also build communities where the story can be experienced as well as told. Just so is community formed and faith communicated—a faith that is pragmatic rather than theoretical, that is transformational rather than soothing (analgesic), that is focused on concern for others rather than on doctrinal (or biblical) correctness. We cannot communicate hope or love or commitment or faith by discussing them as disinterested intellectual concepts aimed at the mind. To truly communicate we must speak to the heart. Communication that has power, that touches the emotions, comes primarily through actions or shared personal stories.

Archbishop William Temple, one of Anglicanism's strongest biblical scholars and theologians, describes revelation in this way. What is revealed in scripture is not propositions about God; rather what is revealed is the person of God. I would add, the way we know a person is through stories, which explains why the Bible is primarily a collection of stories. One of the beauties of this book is the number of stories that touch the heart and in doing so, stretch the mind and motivate the person.

Wisdom is the combination of sound learning in dialogue with reflection on experience. At the heart of wisdom is the ability to endure and even flourish in the midst of ambiguity. This ability may well be the primary difference between wisdom and ideology. Ideology wants certainty; it rejects the ambiguity of "both/and" for the certainty of "either/or." Wisdom understands complexity and incertitude. This is a wise book. This is a book that does not provide answers; rather it touches the heart and stretches the mind that we may bring our personal experience into the dialogue that leads to wisdom.

Advice (1): Don't read this book from front to end quickly; take time. Savor the stories, be touched by the spirit of openness and love, and then allow the mind to sort through the implications for faith, the church, and the future—both personal and communal.

Advice (2): Read this book with others—a book group, a spouse, at a coffee shop, in a small church related group or class. I find it amazing how reading one story invites us to share our own story, and soon the sharing and conversation becomes rich, meaningful, even transforming.

Advice (3): Enjoy.

Ward B. Ewing
Dean and President, retired
The General Theological Seminary
June 24, 2014

Preface

THE LATE ANTHONY DE Mello, SJ, tells a wonderful little tale about a devout noble woman who is the grand dame of a little village. She attends mass every day. Many of the villagers, who are not so grand, hanging about in the village square, note her hurrying to mass and then hurrying back to her grand house each day; they also take note of the fact that she speaks to none of them.

One day, being a little late, she rushes through the village square to the doors of the church and pushes to get in. The doors don't give; she pushes again; that's when she discovers that the doors are locked. Then she sees that there is a written note tacked to the door. It reads: "I'm out there."

I'm writing this little book to respond to all my earnest Church friends who think the Christian mission is to get people in to the Church, however broadly they may want to define "in to." I mean to suggest that they have the mission exactly backwards.

I've come to this awareness over many years. I'm a "cradle Episcopalian" who went straight from college to seminary to ordination. I was a Parish Priest for ten years. Church was my "business"—whatever that meant. I wasn't exactly sure, but I sure worked hard at it. Teaching responsibilities, classes, visits to Parishioners (hospital and home), administrative duties, sermons and leading worship filled my days; yet even in those days, however dimly, I had some occasional inkling that "my" parishioners had real jobs and worked hard all week; occasionally I felt a little bit bad about haranguing them to attend Church on Sunday—their one day of rest. But I *needed* them to attend on Sunday—and on special days. I remember insisting that all good Episcopalians had to attend Church one Ash Wednesday very early in my days as a Priest; my poor wife, newly pregnant with our first child, dragged herself out for the 7:00 a.m. service. Luckily a caring parishioner stood nearby and helped her sit down to avert passing out, which she was just about to do. *I* needed them to come to Church—how else to justify my work? (Except, mostly, I put it in terms—and believed it myself—of it being *their need* to come to Church.)

By happy accident I found my way out of Parish ministry and into education (Clinical Pastoral Education), where I have spent the last forty plus years. Now, in "retirement"—for the last twelve years—I have been really lucky to be assigned as the "Sunday Supply" priest to a small congregation in a historic community. They have taught me what church is. I offer this book to share some of the good news about church.

Along with this growing awareness has been my awareness also of the kind of "prison" many of my clergy colleagues are in. Briefly put, they are immersed in the busyness of keeping the institution (Church with a capital "C") in business—teaching classes, hosting special events, planning elaborate worship services and sermons. And they *need* people to attend. Soon—and usually very subtly—they begin to believe (or at least to act as if) the institution on the corner of Fourth and Vine has the corner on the truth about god; and, since they have it there, you need to come there to get it.

As De Mello's little parable suggests, "I'm out there!"

And a brief explanation:

The reader will note that I sometimes capitalize "Church" and sometimes refer to "church"; and that I sometimes capitalize "God" and sometimes mention "god." My intent is to make a distinction: between the Institution Church and the Institution's God—each of which seems to allow—perhaps require—definition (structure and creed); and the infinite varieties and manifestations of community (church) and the indefinable power/spirit ("god beyond god"), which seems to me somehow to animate for good all community life.

Acknowledgments

I am grateful to one I sometimes call my "fierce and ferocious friend" (everyone should have at least one) and sometimes call my "theological consultant," Rick Weatherstone. Our discussions never fail to stimulate my theological thinking; and he has read, commented on, and encouraged my sermons and this book.

To my friend, Anne Lane I owe much gratitude for her encouragement and her careful reading of the manuscript, with the many suggestions which have greatly improved the writing.

Great thanks, also, to my long time friend and colleague, Rev. Ward Ewing, for agreeing to read and comment, in his foreword, on my work.

I must also acknowledge my many mentors over the years who have taught me so much: the many CPE Students and counselees who have entrusted me with their stories and their journeys; and in these latter years, the wonderful community of Christ Church in Rugby, TN, whose members have tolerated my developing thinking about god and church as I wrote and presented my weekly homilies.

And one more: as will be evident in the text, the people we usually call "homeless"—the ones I've been privileged to know as neighbors and friends—have taught me much and enriched my life immeasurably.

Chapter 1

Telling Stories (Preaching the Bible)

"Naw, we don't worship the Bible," he said, "but we do believe it is the inspired word of God. So our job as preachers is to take these sacred texts and to make them relevant to our lives today."

"Well," I said, "maybe you could say the same thing about Shakespeare; you know that he and the King James Version sound a lot alike. Sometimes I can't tell them apart. And Shakespeare told some mighty powerful truths in his plays and his sonnets."

"Naw," he said, "definitely not! Shakespeare may be wonderful stuff, but it isn't sacred and isn't inspired by God—at least, not like the Bible is."

"How about Emily Dickinson? I know she doesn't use Elizabethan English, but she conveys some important truth—and considerable beauty (which may be the same thing)—in her poetry."

"I like what little I know about her, but it isn't the Bible! I mean, most Christians (and *even* Episcopalians) say something about the Bible containing all things necessary to salvation. Doesn't that make the Bible special? Unique?"

"Hmmm," I said; "a lot of people are pretty sure that God wrote the Bible; and that does give it pretty high authority. And you may be surprised to know that I can agree that 'god' wrote the Bible. But I would add that a better way to say it is that 'god' *writes* the Bible—or, is still writing the Bible."

"But," he continued, "many (maybe most) reputable biblical scholars say something like 'interpretation is continuing but the canon of scripture is closed'; that does mean, I think, that the canon is special, unique."

"Maybe", I replied, "but I think they are just playing with words. If 'god' is alive, animating all that is, how can we deny that revelation about 'god' is to be found everywhere—in nature, in poetry, in plays and novels and history, and in every aspect of human experience? I believe that the canon is not closed, and never will be. 'God' is continually revealing 'god's' self. And those who would close the canon are sadly depriving themselves of the fullness of the good news that 'god' *is* involving god's self in every aspect of life—all the time and every where—then and now.

"Here's my Easter sermon from a while back; it may illustrate my point:"

A precocious child, she is—or maybe not; maybe she is just like all children before we teach them not to notice what is right there before their eyes.

Here's what she had learned—in church, no less! The good news—the gospel—is that life always triumphs over death: little deaths, big deaths, final deaths. Death is hard, painful, sad, real, for sure—but never the final chapter of the book. New life is the final chapter. That was the good news Jesus put forth. And that's what she had learned.

And here's what she noticed: the preacher and her Sunday School teacher almost always told stories about events that happened two or three thousand years ago.

And here's what she wondered: if it is true that new life always springs forth from death—if that is still true today, why do we only tell stories about new life from way back then? Adam and Eve; Moses, Abraham, Isaac, Jacob, Joseph, Saul, David, Jesus, Peter, Paul. Why get stuck on the story of Jesus' death and resurrection?

If it is still true, why don't we tell stories about resurrections that we can see all around us—here and now?

Spring comes after winter—resurrection.

An alcoholic gets clean and begins a new life of sobriety—resurrection.

A man bereft of family and friends, addicted and homeless gets into a program that provides him a community of friends and a place to live—resurrection.

A spouse in a fit of anger berates and belittles his wife; he is remorseful and she forgives; the relationship is restored—resurrection.

A man convicted of homicide by drunk driving, even in prison reforms his life and attends AA meetings, speaks to high school gatherings about drinking and driving and about alcoholism—resurrection.

Metaphor. She may not know the word yet, but like all children, she gets the concept; metaphor is the way children live their lives. So: she understands that we celebrate Jesus' resurrection, because it is a metaphor for how life is—for you and for me and for every body—always—and every where—continually resurrected.

Happy Easter.[1]

"So, you seem to be proud of that sermon," he said. "But I can't tell from it if you believe Jesus rose from the dead."

I thought it best to leave that alone.

But I did add, "Since we were talking about the Bible, here's one I preached on 'How to read the Bible'":

Grampa told lots of stories; in fact, that's about the only way he communicated anything he had to say.

One fine day, as they were sitting in the side yard, under the big oak tree, Timmy asked, "Grampa, how come you tell so many stories?"

"I'll tell you why, but first, bring me some water from the well over there, would you please?"

Timmy came back with the dipper full of cool well water.

"Thanks", said Grampa, "but all I asked for was water; why'd you bring the dipper?"

"Why, to hold the water", said Timmy.

"Of course", said, Grampa; "I have to have something to hold the truth in, too; stories are my dipper."

If I were to title this sermon today, it would be, "How to read the Bible." I think of this connection this morning, because as I was reading the story of God sending the Hebrew people into exile, I thought that so commonly what all of us tend to do with Bible stories is to take

---

1. Easter, 2011

a particular story as referring only to one particular time or event or person or people—in other words, we literalize it. For instance, in today's readings it is easy to believe that God's choosing to both punish and then relieve the Jewish people refers only to a specific people in a specific time and place in history—that is, that it is only about God's saving the Jewish people from their exile.

The beautiful Jeremiah passage is poetic in its imagery of those who had been bad rulers of Israel and those foreigners who carried the Jewish people into exile into Babylonia, and it does refer to a particular ugly and harsh period in Jewish history; Jeremiah then imagines a time to be coming when those evil shepherds will be routed and "I myself," God says, "will gather the remnant of my flock out of all the lands where I have driven them and I will bring them back to their fold, and they shall be fruitful and multiply."

Each story, of course, contains the truth, like the dipper contains a little bit of water; and the Bible itself contains the truth, but there is infinitely more water than the dipper can hold, and the truth is infinitely larger than any one story—or even the whole of the Bible—can hold. Grampa knew that. He was content to tell a story, trusting Timmy to see that it contained a larger truth—that the story is never just the story.

And, in truth, stories always contain larger truth, if we read them rightly; and the Bible always does, if we read it rightly; for each story is a small container of the infinitely, immeasurably, larger truth of the way god is always working. God is always both fully involved in what we label and experience as "evil"—god sent the Israelites into exile—and always fully involved in providing the ultimate relief—god brings them home again to be fruitful and multiply.

Another way we misread the Bible is when we "reify"—that is, to "thingify" God—to make God into a thing or an object or a being—one thing among other things—one being among other beings (another form of literalism).

And though many people read the Bible as proclaiming God to be person or object or thing, that is not the only way to read the Bible. A better way is to see that the Bible is describing the way of the universe—the long arc of history—in which there is always unavoidable pain and suffering and all kinds of trials and tribulations which we, the human race, both cause and suffer in this life. Jeremiah, rightly read, is one such description of the way of the universe.

But, rather than reading the promise of Jeremiah today to restore justice and righteousness as foolishness and blind optimism in the face of blatant misery, or as pertaining only to the Jews—the plain intent of the whole of the Bible is to maintain precisely that the good news is for all people, everywhere and for all time. It is everywhere to be seen—and the news is that god is in the midst of the worst of times and the best of times and that goodness and justice and mercy and peace will always ultimately prevail. Every particular story is a story of a particular instance of misery overcome and goodness prevailing. The Jews are restored from exile to their homeland. And each story proclaims the same universal good news that good always overcomes evil.

"Well, Grampa, is that true?" Timmy asked. "Is it true that there will always be a good end to the story?"

"What do you think?" asked Grampa.[2]

Chapter 2

God

"BUT," HE WENT ON, "*you* said that God is writing the Bible; so you do believe in God?"

"Well", I replied, "of course you couldn't see my quotation marks around the term 'god'; I think of 'god' as a convenient name—shorthand, if you will—for whatever (or whoever) might be thought of as the animating spirit of all that we usually call 'creation'.

"I certainly don't believe in a LARGE BEING 'up there' or 'out there' somewhere. If we want to know what 'god' is 'up to' we'll want to study science and literature and history and economics; I guess you might call this 'natural theology'. A philosopher named Teilhard de Chardin had a notion that everything is in god and god is in everything. 'Panentheism' is the technical term for the belief that god is both all there is and, also, what he called *the omega point*—that is, the end and aim toward which all is moving. So—yes, I believe in god (as process—of which all of us are a part) and no, I don't believe in God as A Being.

"Here's a sermon that may help illustrate my meaning—about some folks who may not believe in God, but who clearly are open to mystery and to the possibility of what I call an animating spirit or principle."

The year is 1977: Jimmy Carter began his term as President; Apple was incorporated; the TV miniseries "Roots" aired on ABC; Queen Elizabeth celebrated her silver anniversary; New York City had a major blackout; Elvis Presley died at age forty-two; the first woman Episcopal Priest was ordained; Apple II—the first personal computer—came on the market; the last Mary Tyler Moore show and the first *Loveboat* show were broadcast; the minimum wage went from $2.50 to $3.35; and Voyager 1 and Voyager 2 were launched.

Most of those items are history—past. Women are still being ordained in the Episcopal (and other) denominations, and the Voyagers are still alive and well—and voyaging ever deeper into space.

Here's my text for today: "No matter what you think you know, what there is to learn is even more interesting." I'm going to do something this morning that I do regularly but rarely admit to openly—I'm going to talk about something I know very little about.

My text is a quote from Dr. Ed Stone, chief scientist for the Voyager project. He told of how Voyager 1 has been moving ever closer to the boundary between our solar system and the space beyond. And a recent report is that all indications are that Voyager 1 has indeed now left our solar system and begun its journey in interstellar space—thirty-seven years after launch! And Dr. Stone and the other developers of the Voyager project (who were all young men then) are very excited. After thirty-seven years, they have finally reached their goal of being able to explore interstellar space itself!

The Voyager spacecraft are expected to continue to function until 2020 and maybe as long as 2025. Stone said that in the Voyager mission, every day seems to bring a new revelation. "No matter what you think you know," he said, "what there is to learn is even more interesting."

Now, switch to another era entirely: the year is maybe 1 or 2 in what is now known as the Common Era. Three scientists from the part of the world where science was then thriving are studying the stars; they spot one they've not seen before, and, being scientists, they naturally want to do what they can to understand this new phenomenon; they follow where it seems to be leading. "No matter what we think we know," they surely said to themselves, "what there is to learn is even more interesting." And so they followed the star. We can wonder about details of the story as we have it in Matthew, or we can be skeptical of what seems to be a fantastic story from what we mistakenly think of as the "pre-scientific era" or we can marvel at the truth in the story of three wise men following their star and letting it lead them to a new awareness of meaning.

I'm currently three fourths of the way through an intriguing book whose title is *Quantum Questions*; it is edited by a fellow named Ken Wilber, a speaker, writer, and philosopher of science. What Wilber does in this book is to select portions of the philosophical musings of some of the brightest scientific minds of the twentieth century. You'll know for sure that I'm way beyond my depth as I name them: Heisenberg (the "uncertainty principle"); Schroedinger (the "wave equation"); Einstein the "theory of general relativity"); de Broglie ("matter waves"); Jeans (a philosopher of science); and Eddington (the theoretical physics having to do with stellar systems). To vastly oversimplify, what Wilber is presenting is these scientists as "mystics"—as musing on meanings beyond their scientific knowledge. While not denying what they know, each in this book is speculating that there is meaning and order underlying all that they have discovered. I believe that none of them claimed to be a Christian; I think each would identify himself truly as an a-theist (note that I mean "a" and not "anti")—that is, as ones who really don't know but who would absolutely agree with Dr. Stone that "No matter what you think you know, what there is to learn is even more interesting."

I am more and more enamored of what I have learned to call "epistemic humility"—a big word to acknowledge how little we know. But the upside of such humility is that it allows us to be always open to the leading of the star: three wise men in the beginning of our modern era—six wise men of the twentieth century—and Voyager and its crew today. "We don't know," say all these scientist/mystics, "but we are in awe of the beauty of the mystery and we dare follow where it leads."

At the risk of trivializing the wonder and the beauty, I dare say that Jesus would happily join himself to this company. He knew what he knew, just as I know what I know and you know what you know; and just as those six great scientists know what they know. An alternate Gospel reading for today tells of Jesus at twelve years of age conversing with the doctors of religion in the Temple. So he knew what he knew, but what's more important, he believed that what is yet to know is even more mysteriously beautiful; and that his mission was to invite us all to dare open ourselves to the awe of the beauty of the mystery. Like Voyager 1, we don't know what's out there; Jesus invites us, in the words of another great mystic, Dame Julian of Norwich, to trust—the operative word—trust that we can go into the farthest and darkest places, trusting that "all shall be well, and all shall be well, and all manner of things shall be well."[3]

"So," he continued, not ready to give up, "those scientists may not be Christians; ok, I get that. But I want to ask you: what do *you* make of the Incarnation?"

3. 2 Christmas, 1/5/14

Chapter 3

"God was in this place and I did not know it"

Gen 28:16

"Aннн, тне incarnation," I said; "that wonderful truth that the church named—and has never understood! The Church has insisted on locating God in human form in one person—Jesus. And all it succeeded in doing was making up a preposterous superman—or super something, since, if he didn't 'sin,' he certainly isn't human. God inhabits everything and every one; if we can speak in any meaningful way of God, we must speak of God incarnate—enfleshed—in each one of us and in every part of what we (again in shorthand) call 'creation'—that is, in every part of all that is, recalling Chardin's idea. And that means, by the way, that the Church doesn't 'own' incarnation; and the Church doesn't have the Jesus franchise. Or, as I like to say to Church people, 'Jesus has left the building.'

"Here's a poem I wrote as my Christmas sermon a while back:"

A Christmas Poem

A great wide gap there came to be
(Or so the story goes)
When humans chose to separate

And treat our God as foe.
It makes a great poetic image
And dramatizes well
The sense we have in this old world
How things have gone to hell.

But poetry carries its own truth
And it can never be
Read by those uncouth
Who read it literally.

The story means to dramatize
The beauty that is now
By contrasting far the size
And darkness before, and how
It took God's own move toward
Our imagined separate fate
To restore the fractured world
To its united state.

How better dramatize this mirth
Than a tale of incarnation
Of God himself in human birth
In a tiny distant nation?

As drama it is glorious
The truth it captures, true
Of God's own perfect harmony
With the likes of me and you.

The Truth's a bit more plain:
'tis now and ever done.

The story's simply to proclaim
That we and God are one.[4]

"Or," I said, "see what you think of this sermon."

Years ago, my wife Helen had surgery to replace a knee joint. Once she was back home, I became, by necessity, the cook. Our daughter, Kate, came for a visit a few days later, and I reported that her Mom was not

4. Christmas 2012

eating very much. She said, "Dad! Look at that plate! You just glop some food on it . . . it certainly doesn't look very appetizing; in fact, it looks terrible!" So I learned to arrange the food attractively on the plate and even, perhaps, occasionally to put a sprig of parsley on it. I won't say—as some might—that presentation is everything. But I certainly learned that it is not unimportant.

I recently saw a very touching brief video interview with the actor Dustin Hoffman, in which he was talking about making the movie, *Tootsie*. You may recall that the movie has Hoffman playing the part of a very difficult male actor, Michael Dorsey—a really good actor, but so demanding and such a perfectionist that directors will no longer hire him. Desperate to get work, Michael decides to dress and make up as a woman; he becomes Dorothy Michaels, and he gets a part in a soap opera as a hospital administrator. Instead of playing one more subservient female (as the script originally called for), Hoffman, as Michael, now Dorothy, portrays the woman as a strong woman who is unafraid to confront her insensitive boss, the chief administrator. She champions the women where she works and women's causes, generally; and, as Dorothy, he becomes the star of the soap opera. Women fans love Dorothy; they love her toughness and straightforwardness. They feel like she is speaking for them.

Tootsie is billed as a comedy, and it has many hilarious twists and turns in the plot, as you might imagine—or remember.

But, in this brief interview, Hoffman says that this movie was never a comedy for him.

Here's how he explained it: he says a long-time and close friend asked him one time, "how would it be different if you'd been born a woman?" Hoffman said that started a long thought process for him which ultimately led to the making of the movie. Once the idea was germinated, he said he went to Columbia Pictures to ask if they'd spend the money to make him up and dress him to look like a woman; he said he would not make the movie unless he could walk down the streets of New York without calling any attention to himself as a cross dresser or any kind of freak.

When he was made up, he looked, and saw that he really did look like a woman and then what struck him was how unattractive he/she was. So he said to the makeup people, "now make me a beautiful woman." He said that they said back to him, "This is the best we can do with what you bring us; this is as good as it gets . . . Charlie." And Hoffman kind of laughed, as he recounted that. And he said, "then I had an epiphany". Later, telling his wife about it, he said, "I have to make this movie." "Why?" she asked.

He said, "Because I think I'm an interesting woman when I look at her on screen; and I realized that if I met her at a party, I'd never talk to her, because she isn't physically attractive". And he choked up as he said, "I realize there are too many interesting women I've not known, because I've been brainwashed . . ."

Now this is not meant to be a politically correct sermon about how our society makes women sex objects.

It is a sermon about presentation—both the making of it and the receiving of it.

When we baptize a baby here, we parade her down the aisle and present her to her new family; and everybody gives their blessing in ooh's and aah's. When we have a wedding, after making it legal and blessing it, I present the couple to the congregation, and they bless it with cheers and applause. When an actor gets an Oscar, he is presented to the audience who cheer and applaud.

My point is simple; one of the things we do when we want to mark any occasion as significant—we have a presentation—we make a big to-do. And it is right that we do that. "Pay attention here," we are saying. And it is the paying attention part that I'm focusing on here. As Dustin Hoffman learned, there's more to it than the presentation; that is only half of the business. The other half is the reception.

In fact, in the Gospel reading for today, the fact that Jesus is brought to the temple to be presented is stated rather matter-of-factly. It is simply the routine—the expected; it is what every Jewish family did. The story spends much more print time on the reception of the presentation. "I've waited all my life to see this; now I can die in peace", says Simeon, and he blesses the child, saying to Mary, "this is a very special child . . ." The woman prophet, Anna, speaks to the whole crowd gathered there that day, about the great things the child will accomplish.

What Dustin Hoffman learned in the making of *Tootsie*, is that no matter how powerful and interesting a woman Dorothy may have been, if he wasn't open to engaging her, he would deprive himself of the opportunity to know and enjoy the person who was there. In the movie, Dorothy was a powerful and in every way fascinating woman, but as anybody who remembers what Dustin Hoffman looks like, she was not beautiful in the accepted sense of that day's fashion. Yet she was exceedingly attractive as a person.

Hoffman did not put it this way—and might not even now—but I'll suggest that what he learned is that god is everywhere presenting herself—everywhere. In all kinds of guises and disguises—in all kinds of circumstances and places—god is constantly presenting herself to us. I mean, Dorothy opened some eyes and set some people free—just like god is supposed to be always doing.

So the issue is not whether Dorothy is there. The issue is whether we are paying attention.

And when we do pay attention—when we look and listen and engage with Dorothy, we are the richer for it—we are blessed. "Wow! I've been waiting all my life to see her . . ."

"So", said Sarah, who had been listening carefully to this sermon, "Preacher, I'm a little unclear here; are you talking about Dorothy or about god?"

"Yes," said the Preacher.[5]

5. Presentation of Christ in the Temple—2/2/14

Chapter 4

Our Brother—He's One of Us

"You don't believe in the divinity of Jesus?" he asked. "I mean, why do you say you don't accept that Jesus was without sin?"

I was quiet for a while, thinking. Then I said, "I'm not trying to *de*-mote Jesus; I am trying to *pro*-mote us—it's more like I'm suggesting the 'divinity' in each of us. Jesus is just like you—and me—a human being. That's a good thing—being human, I mean. I am not alone in noting that it is not at all clear that Jesus ever claimed special or unique status for himself. He seemed content to be who he was, namely, a Rabbi who believed the power of god resided in him—*and in each of us*. It seems to me that the only thing Jesus ever got mad about was all those 'Churchy' people of his day who kept trying to define the rest of us as less than—as deficient, fallen—as 'bad'. Sin is a lawyer's invention."

"So Jesus is not messiah?"

"Sure he is; and so are you: no less anointed than he! Recall what I said about incarnation. Here are three sermons I've recently preached; they may help explain what I'm trying to say about Jesus."

Sermon 1:

A little squib of a headline in *The Christian Century*—a magazine I no longer subscribe to—I mean the very title, *The Christian Century*, seems to me somewhat presumptuous and possibly a little arrogant, since we are either fast approaching or already in what many call the "post-Christian era". I hope that idea that we're in the post-Christian era is not upsetting. I think it is the best news possible if it is true that the Christian enterprise is disestablished—or, as the term is now, no longer "privileged."

Well, that was a long excursion. I haven't even told you yet what the headline said. It said something like, "it is more important than ever that we know who Jesus is." I guess the article, which I didn't read, is responding to the Gospel lesson for today in which Mark tells us that Jesus asks his followers who others say he is; then he goes on to ask, "well, what do you say?"

For years I've pondered that very question (and surely you'd expect no less from a professional Christian); who is Jesus? By the way, you should rejoice that you are amateur Christians; it is we professionals who tend to need to maintain our privileged status; you are free of that.

So, who is Jesus? One thing that will surely be no surprise to you is captured in one of those paraprosdokians, uttered by George Bernard Shaw, that goes like this: "God created man in his image; and then man returned the favor." Which is to say that it is no secret that every age and society imagines Jesus in ways which fit that age and society— we create Jesus. There was a time when I thought that was not a good thing—when I hoped that, in time, I would come to know the essence of the real Jesus. I'll say more about this in a bit, but recall that Sherlock Holmes story I told you a few weeks ago, in which the punch line had to do with how Watson missed what was so obviously present before his very eyes.

I do know that I have assaulted my theological consultant more than once with my continuing questions about who Jesus was/is. And one thing is apparent: one way or another, Jesus has managed to keep in the forefront of the attention of millions of people over a couple of thousand years. That, in itself, invites lots of interesting speculation and discussion.

What I've tended to do with this passage from Mark is to assume that Peter had the answer. I'm pretty sure that is what Mark intended us to believe. It is a nice little literary device: Mark sets it up by propos-ing—intimating—a contrast: "those others say . . . but the truth is . . ."

And, in a sense, I suppose it is the truth that Jesus is the Messiah— but not in the way that the Church—the institution—says. The institu-tion wants to make Jesus unique—one of a kind—the only anointed one—anointed, as you know, is what "messiah" means. Many, many of our hymns suggest this perspective; one comes immediately to mind (without my even looking at the hymn book) "At the Name of Jesus every knee shall bow . . ." I say to you, beware of any hymn or doctrine that suggests that Jesus is more unique than any other individual— than any of you. I'm recalling here George Orwell's *Animal Farm* in which he has one of the characters declare that "All animals are equal, but some animals are more equal than others." His point was, of course, that one enduring human tendency is to want to claim special status for one's self—or one's group.

And the Church has claimed that special status for Jesus—and, by extension, of course, for itself. But, thanks be to God, the Church is losing its special status.

Well, back to the Sherlock Holmes allusion: the plain truth right in front of our noses is that Jesus really meant the question as a straight-forward one. He meant that each and every one of us has to do business with the question. No trick is intended, and no answer already assumed. Who do you say that Jesus is? Who is Jesus for you?

I think that is more than a little liberating; it says that Jesus thinks we can be trusted to think for ourselves and to respond with integrity to what we read and hear and see all around us. And I think that is because Jesus knew himself to be a man who was free. He was free to think for himself—which is surely how he knows that you and I are free. We, too, are free to think and to be: to live out, as he did, what it means to be anointed—a messiah.

It is a freedom that sometimes enables us to do heroic things. With the 9/11 anniversary fresh in our minds, we recall the many deeds of heroism in which people went beyond themselves to save others—as if inspired—anointed for the task.

So dare we say that those who attacked the hijacking pilots and brought their flight crashing to the ground in Shanksville, Pennsylvania—dare we call them saviors—dare we think they were messiah— anointed? Am I suggesting that the woman on the 90th floor of the world trade tower who helped others out to the stairway and lost her own life in the process is a savior—a messiah?

Or, maybe, a less dramatic example: some time ago I told you about one of our homeless neighbors who was one of our early success stories—he sobered up after years of drinking and was able to move into our permanent, supportive housing complex. I'll call him Sam. Well, some time ago, now, Sam fell off the wagon again—badly—so bad that he had to be evicted. Another of our neighbors I've mentioned—Billy, who befriended me when I was a new, green volunteer, now does live in that complex and works in our building helping to keep it clean. Thursday, Sam came into our counseling area, late in our day; he looked terrible. Billy was there, getting ready to begin his cleaning chores. For a while he sat beside Sam in our lobby and talked to him. I was very moved by his tender attention and obvious care for Sam. After Sam left, I told Billy how much I appreciated him; he told me how he tries to help Sam out—he told me that the night before he had promised to meet Sam to help him go buy some groceries, but that he had found Sam under the bridge, passed out with drink, so he let him be. Undeterred, however, he promised to take him shopping that next evening.

Am I calling Billy a savior—messiah? Yes.

And am I suggesting that you are messiah? Anointed? You know I am. And, at the same time you are the savior, you are also the saved.

You are unique—there is only one you. Yet you have something in common with every other unique you: you—we—are both the one saved and the one saving. Just like Jesus—we're anointed—and free to find out and to live out what that means.

How can this be? And if it is true that we are anointed, is that good news?

Don't ask me; ask yourself. I say you're anointed. What do you say?[6]

Sermon 2:

I heard Jesus the other day on the radio.

He said that, as the public defender in Knoxville, he had done his best for a defendant but had lost the case. His client was convicted. He didn't give the details, but it was apparently a serious crime.

"Anyhow," Jesus said, "I was packing up my briefcase, preparing to leave the courtroom when the client said he had to talk with me right then. I thought to myself, 'here's a man who knows that he will probably die in prison; the least I can do is listen to him for a few minutes.' So he put down his briefcase and turned to the man who said to him, simply, 'Never in my life has anyone fought for me like that. Thank you.'"

"He thanked me," said Jesus; and Jesus wept.

In talking about his work as public defender, he commented on the importance of respect; he said he wanted the attorneys in his office

6. 16 Pentecost; 9/16/12

to be competent in the law, but also compassionate, empathic, non-judgmental and loving—loving the client so as to empower him to get his life together. Empowering—respecting—loving.

That's what Jesus talked about on the radio show. And, he illustrated it with that story of the client he had respected enough to fight for with all he had.

And then yesterday in the *Knoxville News Sentinel*, I read about Jesus, a Youth Service Officer in Jefferson County. She works with truant high school students, and she noticed that the truancy rate was not being affected at all by fines and community service programs that the court was imposing. All on her own, she recruited Carson-Newman University students. Their qualification had to be that they had experienced some adversity in their own lives. And the students functioned simply as coaches and cheerleaders to those students they were assigned to work with. Jesus created something she called the "Journey Program" to teach children how to deal with cliques, friends and low self-esteem as well as teaching accountability for their actions. Since 2009, ninety-three students have graduated the Journey Program, and only eleven have returned to Juvenile Court for an offense after graduation.

And Jesus came into the Volunteer Ministry Center Refuge lobby the other day. She was probably about fifty; she hadn't had a bath in a while. Whoever she was talking to as she came in was not visible to me. Then she came up to me and in rather halting and garbled speech, she told me she wanted to get a bus ticket to "go to the coast". It was all pretty confused. Then, Jesus' sister, one of our volunteer counselors, who was standing near by, said, "I'll talk to her." I guess they spent an hour talking together. We could not help her get to "the coast." As she was leaving, we invited her to come back after lunch to make some long distance calls on our phone. She never came back.

Pick up your bulletins and follow along as I read the first sentences from the lesson from Hebrews: "Let mutual love continue. Do not neglect to show hospitality to strangers, for by doing that some have entertained Jesus without knowing it. Remember those who are in prison . . . those who are being tortured . . ."

Remember that Jesus said that respect makes all the difference. I guess he meant that that's how you show love.[7]

7. 15 Pentecost; 9/1/13

Jesus Has Left the Building

Sermon 3

Once upon a time, several years ago, Jesus came to have a drink with me on our front porch in Durham, North Carolina. He came in the person of a fellow named Lex Mathews.

We had known Lex for some time; he was an Episcopal Priest in the Diocese of North Carolina when we were living in Durham, and I was serving as the Episcopal Chaplain and Clinical Pastoral Educator at Duke Hospital.

Lex had been a college campus Chaplain at UNC in Chapel Hill; he had also served in that role in Florida. Lex also loved sailboats; and at one time he tried to make it as a charter boat captain. If I remember rightly, he had bought and massively rebuilt a big old wooden sailboat (no "Tupperware"—as he called plastic boats—no Tupperware for him). I don't know the details, but that plan didn't work out. I think it was at that point that the Bishop of North Carolina, Tom Frazer (known for being often wrong but never in doubt), Tom called Lex to become the Director of Christian Social Ministries for the Diocese—called him to do the kind of work that Jesus always does.

So Jesus/Lex would hear about some kind of good work that combined resources (including, most importantly, people) with a community need. Think, for example, church sponsored and church run soup kitchens; they were a hot new thing (at least in North Carolina) in the mid-1970s.

Lex was old shoe, low-key, and a friend to everybody—and he knew everybody. He traveled around the diocese; he'd call up a friend in one of the churches in the diocese and say, "Hey, let's go to lunch." And they'd chit-chat a while and then he'd tell his friend about some good idea he'd heard about—for example, he might say, "what do you know about soup kitchens?" And before long Jesus would have him not only interested, but also excited about the idea. Why he might even entice him to agree to gather a few other possibly interested folks over to his house just to explore the idea.

And, of course, Jesus' gentle, low-key friendliness doesn't mean that he doesn't have great and deep insight into his friends. It didn't take him long to really get to know you—know who you are; know what your interests and abilities are; and always with the sense that he not only knows you well, but he really likes who you are.

So one evening Jesus invited himself over to our house; he sat on our front porch on one fine spring evening, drank my scotch and we schmoozed a while and then he asked, "what do you know about hospice?" Well, being a hospital chaplain, I had heard of it; it was a fairly new thing developing in England in the 1970s—with maybe one or two hospices in this country. I allowed that I knew just enough about it to be interested.

Well, that's all it took, and I don't need to belabor the point; you get the drift. Before very long, Lex called together a few other people and got us to talking about hospice. Those were the days when there was money available (either that or Lex had something on the bishop); anyhow, soon Lex had pulled together some money and got Helen and me and two others to fly off to Boonton, New Jersey, to a conference on hospice.

Before I knew what was happening, I was the President of Hospice of North Carolina, Incorporated—a longer and more impressive name than its then very brief history.

And the great thing about Jesus is that he is so certain that you can do the job that you come to believe it yourself.

And Jesus isn't one of these crusaders whose only interest in you is as a potential recruit for one of his projects. No—the first thing about Jesus is that he really knows you and he really likes you. He really knows you—so he can invite you into a work that really fits you—a work that gives you life.

Now here's another similar Jesus story: this time Jesus is walking with his friends through a foreign territory; the friends go off to town, leaving him to sit down for a rest by a well. This was back in the days when it was improper for unrelated men and women to speak to one another in public. So a woman from this country comes to the well to get some water; she is surprised that this fellow from another country and another religion would even speak to her, but he does. He asks for a drink. She gives him one. She sits down and they begin to talk. Before long, they got to talking about religion. One way or another, she began to reveal things about herself. And he responded in such a way as to let her know that he got it—he understood her story and seemed to accept it and her fully, as friend and colleague. She was so impressed by his knowing and accepting her that she went back to her village to tell everybody about her experience. "Hey," she said, "I met this man and told him all about myself, and I had this wonderful sense that he both knew me and loved me just as I am." And her fellow villagers were so impressed that they invited him to come stay with them for a while so they could become friends, too.

Now John, in our Gospel reading for today, is so busy asserting—trying to prove—the divinity of Jesus (why he makes it sound like Jesus is some kind of mind-reader)—so busy proving Jesus' divinity that he misses the point of his own story.

It's a simple story really—about two people having a drink together—two people meeting. Over the drink and over time (John conflates it into one dramatic encounter, but really its over time), the people get to know each other; they become friends. Like Lex—and the people he befriended.

And then good things happen.[8]

8. 3 Lent, 2014; the reference is to John 4:5–42

Chapter 5

Sin? Evil? Who's to Blame?

"ALL RIGHT," HE SAID, warming to the task. "You want to promote me to messiah status and you want to give Shakespeare and Emily Dickinson—and who knows who all else—equal status with the Bible. So what about sin? And what do you mean about sin being a lawyer's invention?"

"Sin?" I asked, perplexed. "Where exactly does that question come from?"

"Well, I'm just wondering where in your thinking is evil located? I mean people suffer and die. There are earthquakes and tsunamis—'natural disasters'; and there are murders and torture and rape and wars—'man-made disasters'. How do you explain all those; and who do you blame?"

"Oh," I said, "you're looking for someone to blame; somebody's responsible for making bad stuff happen, right? That's why I mentioned lawyers."

"Right! Now you're getting somewhere. Humans—you and I—are responsible for the bad stuff—we're guilty; in traditional language we are fallen creatures in a fallen world; that's what the Church means when it says we are sinners."

Again, I paused, thoughtful. "Well, here are a couple of ideas. One: how about we blame god for all the bad stuff? I mean, we want to claim god as the first cause, the creator of all. So doesn't it stand to reason that if god gets credit for the 'good' stuff, god also gets to take blame for the 'bad' stuff (if such there be)? But then, two: what do you make of all the good things that humans do? I mean, Tom murders Joe, but Sue rescues Tony from his homeless drunken state and gets him sober, employed, and housed."

"Whoa, now; you're moving too fast. Blame God? God is good; it is you and I who have gone bad—we're the sinners. Remember Adam and Eve? They had it made and they rebelled. Sue rescued Tony, because she allowed herself to be open to the inspiration of God the Holy Spirit to do that good work—God gets the credit; but Tom murdered Joe, because Tom is a sinner—a rebel against God's goodness—Tom gets the blame."

"Then how about this?" I suggest. "How about the notion that no one is to blame. Maybe what we have labeled 'evil' and what we have labeled 'good'—all of it is simply part of the natural order of things—the way things are."

Chapter 6

Salvation: Who Needs It?

"CHAOS! CHAOS!" HE SHOUTED. "There's got to be some order in this universe. The Church didn't create sin; it just describes the nature of human nature—sinful, fallen. The law may punish sinful behavior, but the Church is in the business of converting people—turning them from their wickedness, offering them some guidance for living right, saving them."

"Of course," I said, calmly, "if people are just being themselves—just being who they are—and behaving the way people behave—or, as you might say, acting as they were 'created' to act—then they don't need saving, because they are already exactly who 'god' created them to be. Or as the Tao Te Ching suggests, the world is sacred—perfect—as it is."

"Then," he said, perplexed, "what is the need for the Church?"

The way he said it caused me to picture the words, "THE CHURCH" in gothic bold italics, and all capital letters.

I let that question hang in the air.

Chapter 7

Church and Sacraments

"Let me try again," he said. "Church both reminds people of their sinfulness *and* provides them a way out."

"That reminds me," I replied, "of a very old joke. A fellow who is quite drunk boards a Greyhound bus for a long journey; as the bus is driving down the road, he begins to tear his newspaper into bits; then he opens the window and begins tossing the bits out. His seatmate is incredulous. 'What on earth are you doing?' he asks. 'Shhh', says the drunk; 'I'm keeping the elephants away.' The seatmate looks out the window. 'I don't see any elephants,' he says. 'Works every time,' says the drunk."

"Listen," he said. "People need to come to Church. They need the sacraments of Baptism and Holy Communion; Baptism to make them members of God's own body and Communion to nourish the body."

"Sacraments—they belong to the Church?"

"Well, yes!"

"That reminds me of an old joke; a fellow who was quite drunk . . ."

"Don't start with that joke again," he said.

"Well, okay," I replied. "Sacrament is simply a word used to describe the natural order of things; God inhabits and expresses God's being and meaning in and through stuff—humans, ideas, frogs, algae, molecules, neurons, mathematics, poetry, and on and on. Even the Church comes close to stumbling on the truth about sacraments (and the truth that sacraments don't belong to the Church) when it calls marriage a sacrament. Physical stuff expresses spiritual reality: for example, it takes a body to make—that is, to create—love. A fellow named von Hugel used to say something like, 'I kiss my daughter because I love her, and I kiss my daughter in order to love her.' Sacraments are not Church property. Sacraments describe the way 'god' behaves in the world; or, as I would rather say it, the way the natural order behaves. The beauty and the majesty of that mystery we call 'god' is embedded, inherent, incarnated in all that is—in every idea—in every emotion—in every physical thing and in every community—including in us: in you and in me. And it *is* mystery: we can never comprehend it, but we can sure enjoy it."

Chapter 8

Church Out There

"So, you *do* believe in Church," he declared, triumphantly.

"Oh, yes," I said. "She gave birth to me." And I thought to myself, but didn't say just then, that the time comes when each of us has to grow up and separate from mother; we may remain friends, but now as equals and no longer in a hierarchical relationship.

"So, what is your objection to trying to get people to come to Church?"

"Let me tell you a story," I said. "I was at a convention some years ago; after the afternoon-long business session, we had a break and then the convention banquet. The East Tennessee State University Bluegrass Band provided the entertainment. (This is a group of college kids and their teacher, but they are in no way amateurs.) Now I suspect that Bluegrass is not everybody's favorite—though I truly can't understand how that can be so—but I have to tell you that there's something about bluegrass that stirs my soul and fills me with such joy that I want to cry.

"So—for me just hearing the music was heavenly. Sitting with the other members of our delegation to this convention added to the enjoyment, since they all are fans of bluegrass—so it was a communal experience; our spirits were fed.

"If you've ever watched a bluegrass performance you will have seen what I'm trying to describe: one or another of the band members will take the mike and announce the song; she or he may then lead the opening; soon the guitar player will step back and to the side and the banjo player will step up and play the lead. It looks like a dance. Then the banjo player will step aside and the mandolin will come with its high pitch; he swings away, making room for the violin—one, two, or three of them playing with and against one another. All the while, in the background you can hear and see the big bass player providing the drive and the beat—a leader, perhaps, but a 'servant leader' who is unobtrusive. Then it's back to the guitar—the mandolin comes forward again—and so on. Each is featured for a moment—and truly stars—then to step back—to dance away—so that another shines for a moment.

"What is so beautiful about bluegrass is the way there is such complete cooperation that there is no apparent leader—no, here is a better way to say it: each one is a leader—there is such a sense of community that there is a wordless sharing of the lead role, each taking a turn at the mike, but all playing together; there is always a harmony. And it is very much a dance as each steps up, swings to the music, and then slides back or to the side as another moves in.

"That is church," I declared. "Nobody said 'Jesus' or 'God' or 'Holy Spirit', but they didn't have to. What do you think?"

"What a wonderful story," he said, "just wonderful, but," he paused, "don't you think we want to acknowledge the awesome power of God's Holy Spirit in this event?"

"Why? *Cui bono?*—for whose benefit? Does god need us to acknowledge his (or her) power? Doesn't the good news stand on its own? And, furthermore, wherever community happens, people already know in their hearts that they've experienced a gift: a bluegrass band, a basketball team, a working group in a tire distribution company, a glee club, a sewing circle, a dinner group— you name it. There's an odd little story—it may have been told by Shakespeare, or it may be in the Bible—as I say, I get them mixed up. It's a story about two friends deep in earnest discussion about important events in their lives. A stranger joins them but picks right up on the conversation; they have dinner together. After dinner, the stranger leaves, and they say to one another something like, 'what a wonderful conversation we've had and what deep understandings we've reached and how close we've become. That stranger was like a breath of fresh air; what a great experience.'"

"Whenever and wherever two or three are gathered together in community—there is church—there is where 'god' 'dwells'. So maybe it is more accurate to say that we don't come to church, but rather that church comes to us.

"There was a time when I very much believed that it was our task to get people to come to us. Now, I'm at a point where I'm happy to welcome any one who wants to come any time s/he wants to come. The worship activities of singing, praying, communing are good things *but only for those who find inspiration in them and so want to do them.* To try to persuade, cajole (or 'guilt') people into 'coming to church' totally misses the point.

"Let me say it more starkly," I added, "worship is for those who already belong to the 'club'; others are welcome to attend as often or as seldom as they wish—and to get (take) for themselves whatever they desire. And any who want to 'join' are welcome to do so. By the way, I mean to reframe the use of the word 'club' to make it a good thing—like community—in case that is not already obvious.

"If what we mean by 'church' is community—then there are lots of churches and people usually manage to find a community, or a club, that gives them something of what they are looking for; and, if you pay attention, you can readily see that each church—community—club does have its own 'liturgy.' I had not attended a University of Tennessee football game in years, for example; then, a while back, a friend invited me to join him. The thing that struck me the most was the 'liturgy' that those 'worshippers' all seemed to know: when to stand, when to sit, when to shout. And there certainly was a sense of commonality—community. And, if I want to be part of that club/community, I'll learn the liturgy. Think about how any civic club conducts its meetings, and you'll see liturgy. A community/club creates its own liturgy, just as much as the liturgy creates community; it is 'both/and'.

"I was at a clergy conference recently; we were talking about church, and community, and good news. One of my colleagues told a wonderful story about offering a course to a 'secular' group; he said that it occurred to him to ask some of the participants about their church experience. He said they said to him, 'Oh, we don't have a church; this class is our church.' I thought that was wonderful—they 'got it'—they knew what church was. I almost fell off my chair when the fellow told us that his response was, 'well, we'd better have some worship'. I thought to myself, '*He* doesn't get it; *they* knew that they were 'worshipping'; he was the one who didn't see it.

"Much of the talk at that conference had the unspoken implication that we (the Church—the Clergy) have the franchise on 'true' community; so we never even see that god is in the community building business—that wherever community happens, god is already there doing the work in and through us.

"So we need to be going out there, instead of trying so hard to get them in here."

And I added, "Here's a sermon I preached not long ago about . . . well, you'll see what it is about:"

I attended my local church the other day. When I got there that morning, three ladies were gathered at the communion table preparing the elements. I came up to the table to partake just in time to hear one of the ministers assure one of the others ladies of her prayers. I wasn't privy to the conversation, so I don't know what the prayer request was about, but the warmth and concern amongst the three was obvious. It felt good just to be close.

I go to that church fairly often—often enough that I recognize folks and they recognize me. I go in and over to the communion table—some times I'm the only one there—and I fix my coffee and then go up to the counter where I'm greeted warmly by the chief minister as I pay for my coffee. She recognizes me and I recognize her and we exchange pleasantries; we are glad to see each other. I guess by now that you've gathered that I'm talking about the local convenience store in a neighborhood near my house. As I say, I've attended that church frequently enough that I'm now recognized and welcomed. As I walked out the door and climbed into my truck that morning, I left, feeling the warmth of that little community—I'd been to church and had communion.

Churches are funny places; I mean those groups of people who self-consciously identify themselves as Christian Churches; why, I guess I'm talking about us. And, like any specific group, we can get caught up in our own special language and ways of doing things.

So around here we talk about Advent (with a capital "A")— and we change the color of the altar hangings and we have a special ring of candles to light—one for each Sunday—and we change the words of our formal worship. Now there's nothing wrong with any of this—with the exception that we may so specialize advent that we forget that all advent means is that god is coming to us; all Advent means is that god is always—always—coming to us—to be with us—to share our lives— our sorrows and our joys. I don't know how it works, but there's something empowering, comforting, strengthening, that happens when the community gathers.

So those ladies at the communion table—they didn't have a prayer book and there wasn't a hymn—but, just as promised and just in time, god came to us there, joined us there, was in our midst. We were the community gathered for just a bit, and, just as when people gather around the fire, we were warmed in that brief gathering.

I told you one time about my grandson, Patrick. My son, William, his Daddy, was driving us somewhere and he told Patrick to be on the lookout for a particular landmark they'd been talking about. "My eyes are wide open to see it," said Patrick.

So—this week—this beginning of Advent—if you keep your eyes wide open to see it, you'll surely see god and feel the warmth coming into your midst everywhere you go to gather with others.

Happy Advent.[9]

9. 1 Advent 12/2/13

Chapter 9

The Good News about Sin

"EARLIER," I BEGAN, "YOU were wanting to define us as sinners and sin as related to evil, right?"

"Right," he said; "it is because we are sinners—depraved, fallen from the way God intended us to be—that we do evil deeds to one another—that we rape, pillage, enslave, and murder one another; or, if that's too dramatic for you, we are regularly cruel to one another; we regularly fail to feed the hungry or clothe the naked, or house the homeless, and so on and on," he paused for breath. "Surely you don't deny all the ills that I've named."

"Not at all," I replied, "but I have another story for you:

"I was counseling the other day with a man in his mid-seventies. He said that he and his wife were still learning how to make love. It was a sort of confession he was making to me, since he said that he had some times been cruel to his wife over the years, putting her down, finding things to criticize more than to praise. That was not all there was to their marriage, he said; and she certainly had gotten her licks in on him. He was remorseful, yes. But, perhaps more importantly, he was grateful for their long years together. Here's what he said to me: 'It occurred to me that I could wallow in guilt for all those times I have mistreated her; or, I could celebrate the many, many opportunities I—and we—have had to learn from our mistakes. That's when the thought about our lovemaking occurred to me. At first, as I thought about it, I thought, I wish I had known as a young married man what I know now; and then I thought, that's impossible—the only way we've learned is through all the errors we've made. We can be sad that we are so error-prone; or we can rejoice that each mistake is an opportunity to learn.'"

"Oh, my!" he exclaimed. "You are saying that sin is god's gift to us!"

"You understand me perfectly," I said. "Dame Julian of Norwich and I both think of sin as one of god's greatest gifts."

Chapter 10

The Good News About
the Way of the World

"IT'S ALL ABOUT RECYCLING," I mused.

"What are you talking about?" he asked.

"Oh, did I say that out loud? I was just thinking to myself about my telling you that sin is a good thing; and how it seems that we are able to take something 'bad' and turn it into something 'good'. Or, you probably prefer to say that God takes something bad and turns it into something good. That's why I thought of recycling. Old worn out stuff that's spoiled or broken or used up, gets recycled and made into something new. Or, as the Episcopal prayer book says, 'Things which had grown old are being made new.'

"See what you think of this sermon."

Paraguay is one of the more impoverished countries in South America. The capital city of Ascuncion has a city nearby, actually almost a suburb. The city is named Cateura; it is actually a garbage dump that became a small city—a city which grew up around the dump, because the citizens of Cateura depend on the dump for their livelihood. The dump is the primary garbage dump for the whole country; there is only one crop to harvest in Cateura, and it produces all year long—the crop is trash. The city is populated with people whose only profession is to pick through the trash to find and harvest whatever recyclables they can

35

sell. The trash-pickers (as they are known) are mostly peasant farmers who migrated to Cateura after having been displaced from their land by large landowners. The city is a slum and a dump, with very little electricity, with little or no sanitation, and with a contaminated water supply.

There is little or nothing for the children who live there to do; many become delinquent and join gangs and roam the streets. They are forgotten children.

Into this misbegotten world came a man a few years ago—a man named Favio Chavez; it is not clear to me how or why he came to this slum city or how he made the decision that he did. What he decided was to start a music school for the children of Cateura. He believed that music would give meaning and joy to the lives of those children.

One real problem right away, as Favio noted, was that a real violin would have cost more than the price of a house in Cateura, and it would have been promptly stolen. There were no instruments and no money to buy them. How to get started?

Somehow, Favio teamed up with one of the trash pickers who was also something of a creative genius, a fellow named Nicholas and known as 'Cola'. Cola worked three days a week harvesting trash to recycle and the rest of the time he was in his workshop. He teamed up with Favio and began to fashion musical instruments.

From an oven tray—though he'd never seen a violin in his life—he made a violin. With an oil drum and some old food utensils, he made a cello. Discarded plastic pipes, and keys and bottle tops became saxophones and trumpets. Two large dessert tins welded together side by side made a guitar. An old X-ray plate became a drum.

Soon there were all the instruments needed to make an orchestra, and Favio had his music school. Little children—ages five, six, seven, and on up—came to school and began to learn to play. Now, some years later, some of the more experienced kids (teenagers) are teaching the younger ones.

An internationally known and talented Paraguayan guitarist named Berta Rojas now lives in Maryland; she regularly flies to Asuncion and goes to Cateura to conduct master classes for these children.

I have to tell you that I cried when I heard the music that those children produced on those ludicrous instruments. Words cannot express the power and the beauty of the children or of their music. A nineteen-year-old boy named Bebi played the Prelude to Bach's Cello

Suite No. 1 on the oil drum cello—and played it beautifully. Who could ever have imagined that an oil drum could make Bach come alive?

Ada's grandmother saw a notice about the school and enrolled her two granddaughters. "I always wanted to be a musician myself," she said, "but since that was not possible for me, that desire will live on and be fulfilled in my grandchildren". Ada, now thirteen, is first chair in what they have named the Landfilharmonic Orchestra and she is one who teaches the little ones. On her makeshift violin she plays with the orchestra a part of Vivaldi's Four Seasons. Again tears came to my eyes at the beauty and the audacious creativity of these children. Ada says that without music her life would not be worth living.

Now I have two texts for this sermon that I wanted to save until the end; they are not from the Bible; one is from the words of that Paraguayan guitarist who now lives in Maryland. She said: "I couldn't believe you could make music with trash".

Or maybe the better text comes from Favio, who says, "You send us garbage, and we send you music."

A news item two days ago on NPR reports that in 2011 there was a massive increase in the absorption of carbon dioxide by the land—scientists noted an area they call a "land sink," where the carbon got sucked up in an amount about 40 percent above what was expected—and the biggest surprise was that it was absorbed by vegetation and land which normally absorbs almost no CO_2. Of course, we all know that carbon is everywhere, and it is constantly cycling through various forms. Our bodies contain carbon. Plants thrive on it—they must have it to live. Big trees absorb huge amounts. That reported massive increase got my attention, because, all of a sudden, it struck me that the very earth we inhabit is in the recycling business. It is as if the earth is saying to us, "you send us CO_2, and we send you life."

"You send us garbage, and we send you music."

The whole earth is in the resurrection business; Favio and the children of Cateura are simply participating—with joy—in the way of the world—carbon dioxide to abundant life—garbage to music.

"You send us garbage, and we send you music."[10]

10. 6 Easter, 5/25/14

Chapter 11

How to Write a Sermon
(In Two Parts)

Begin with a story . . .

Always . . .

Without fail . . .

(*And not a Bible story—never—never—ever—begin with a Bible story!*)

If you cannot find or create a contemporary story that captures something of the good news of God, you haven't yet grasped the good news. And putting forth good news is the one and only purpose of sermon. (And, by the way, Emily Dickinson had it right: the news is so incredibly rich and good and *big* that it can only be approached on the slant; it's too big and bright to look at directly—or to be presented fully in even the most beautifully crafted sermon.)

Humor is always good.

(Of course, you've *looked at* the texts; and they may suggest a message to you, but there's nothing more deadly than a preacher *explaining* or repeating in other words the text which has just been read—nothing more deadly, unless it is the stringing together of several snippets of biblical text, as if the hearers are all biblical scholars and can immediately grasp their current application.)

Epistemic humility is always called for; if you are certain that you know what God means or God wants, you are no better than nor different from the most fundamentalist Muslim or fundamentalist Christian. So tell a story that conveys that you know that we are all just muddling through as best we can, without certainty but with a certain wonder—and maybe a little hope combined with a pinch of trust that life triumphs.

Occasionally, perhaps, you may mention Jesus, but don't overdo it. After all, he's just one of us.

How to write a sermon, part two:

With or without even the germ of an idea, your job is to get started:

Sit down and start to write.

If you are fortunate, you will have a good friend or group of friends whom you trust enough to open up even odd or "crazy" thoughts and ideas; friends may provide the germ or nurture yours—or both.

And as you are writing, listen to yourself; argue with yourself; have second thoughts; engage yourself in dialogue.

There's an old story about a famous sculptor—I forget who it was exactly—who was asked, "How do you do a sculpture of a horse?" He replied, "Easy. Start with a big block of marble and take away everything that doesn't look like a horse." Your sermon will often have lots of material that isn't the horse. Chisel away!

You'll always have something of truth come to you to share.

"The people who have been my best teachers about preaching," I said, "are good old fashioned storytellers. I'll bet you could name any number of novelists, historians, social scientists, or others who begin every chapter with an expertly told story about a contemporary person or event; the story captures your attention and your imagination. Only then might they go on to tease out a truth that the story suggests.

"And I used to tell my students that if their stories were good enough, they might not even have to 'explain' the meaning, since the story would carry its own weight.

"You did get the point of my little story about the drunk and the elephant without my having to explain it, didn't you?

"Well presented material gives me two things: one is seeing that one of the best ways to communicate truth is through good stories expertly told; the other is an increased awareness of and appreciation for the rich variety and depth and breadth and beauty in all that is. Both are crucial to the task of preaching—and note that it is *not* good news if it excludes any of the following: Baptist or Catholic or Muslim or Christian or Jew or Hindu or Buddhist or non-believer—or anybody at all. If what we are all about is telling folks good news—then any story which conveys that sense of goodness is sufficient, and perhaps all the more powerful without the 'explanation'.

"Here's an example: Phil Mickleson, the golfer, is also a devoted family man. Phil really is a good golfer, but he also is a gutsy kind of golfer who will take big risks, and, from time to time, the risk will result in a really disastrous shot. A few years back, he was playing in one of the major tournaments. He took one of those risky shots, and, sure enough, it turned out very badly. He had been in the lead until then, but he gave up the lead and had to settle for being the runner-up.

"Just after he finished, his eight-year-old daughter ran over and snuggled up to him. 'Are you OK, Daddy?'

"'Well, I'm a little disappointed; I'd like to have won that tournament.'

"'Well, second place isn't so bad. Let's go have some pizza.'

"A really good sermon would stop right at this point, because normal folks don't need any prompting or explanation to hear her hope and her trust that the future has a delicious pizza in it. And, if the preacher simply can't stand to trust people that much, he might be allowed to title the story, 'The Little Girl who Believed in the Resurrection'; but I'll lay you odds that most preachers would be certain that they must give 'the moral of the story'. What an insult to the intelligence of their hearers!

"What they need to be doing, instead, is simply telling stories —with a sort of child-like trust that the stories will reveal the god who is in and through and around every story, every event, every person, every*thing—everywhere.*"

"But," he said, "the Gospel is more than a sweet, uplifting story."

"Well, I'm not sure I agree with you," I said, "I think any child, having felt Daddy's 'death'—so to speak—in the loss, will sense the hopefulness in the ending of the story. Good news includes more then the sweet and uplifting, but good news *is* always sweet and uplifting.

"But, if that's too 'sweet' for you, how about this: the characters in this story are three: Amanda Boxtel, an unnamed soldier, and a fellow named Eythor Bender:

"In 1992, Amanda Boxtel, an attractive, athletic young woman, 24 years of age, was skiing; in a freak somersault accident she was, in an instant, paralyzed from her pelvis down. While she was still in the hospital, recovering from the accident, her doctor walked into her room and announced to her that she would never walk again. Boom!

"She has been wheelchair bound for nineteen years, unable to walk. During this time she has not been idle; she has learned to do a remarkable variety of physical activities—even snow boarding—but, true to that doctor's pronouncement, her paralysis has been permanent. She is unable to walk; she has not walked for nineteen years.

"In March of 2011, a researcher named Eythor Bender made a public presentation (which I saw on video) of something he and his colleagues had been working on. He had a fully uniformed and combat equipped soldier come on stage dressed in something I'll call a sort of body suit (but which Bender calls an 'exoskeleton'); it is battery powered and computer driven. The soldier demonstrated how this exoskeleton enabled him to carry much more than the 100-pound pack that soldiers normally carry these days—and to carry it easily, walking, bending, stooping, and twisting with ease, and with no damage to his back. The soldier explained that the computer sensed his movements and enhanced and augmented his strength and agility through the tiny motors at the knees and elsewhere in the exoskeleton.

"Then a very attractive blond woman wheeled on stage in her wheel chair. It was, of course, Amanda, the one who had been told she'd never walk. She wheeled herself near to a chair where was placed another exoskeleton; as all paraplegics do, she had to use her arms to lift one leg and then the other over from the wheel chair so as to place her feet and legs into the leggings of this outfit. Slowly then she stood up; and she walked!—she walked! Something she had not done for nineteen years! Her laughter bubbled right out of her as if from a delighted child getting the best Christmas present ever. She was walking! She laughed right out loud. The audience clapped; and she laughed."

"Do I have to explain that we have just recounted a story about death and resurrection?"

"No; I get that, and it's a nice story—heartwarming, even," he said, "but it is a bit simple; she overcame a physical handicap—a serious and major handicap, to be sure—but a physical thing. I mean, there are what I might call 'wounds to the heart' which can't be repaired. My sister and I had a major falling out years ago; she said some things that can't be taken back; we haven't spoken in years, and I don't think we ever will again."

"Does that make you sad?" I asked.

"A little bit; but that was long ago, and we've moved on."

"You obviously still recall it occasionally; do you wish it were different?"

"I suppose so; but it never will be."

"It might."

"How?"

"Somebody will have to repent."

"Yes!" he said. "She needs to be sorry for what she said; and she's not sorry! And I didn't do anything wrong."

"You've seen that ad on television for one of the mutual fund companies—I forget which one—that shows a broad green stripe moving in front of a couple, illustrating that it is leading people in the right way? It goes for some distance and then makes a sharp turn. The voice-over says, 'turn here'.

"Repent has little or nothing to do with being sorry; it simply means, 'turn here'. So your sister might, some day, turn and take a new direction—or, *you* might. Can you say 'resurrection?'"

Chapter 12

"Tell all the truth, but tell it slant"

"Here's an example," I said, "of presenting the truth in the Bible without quoting the Bible:"

Once upon a time, in a country not too far away, there was a bright young fellow named Thomas Barlow Enright IV. Thomas came from a good home. He had a hard working father, an executive in a large company, who made a good living. His mother stayed at home while he and his siblings were little; then she went to work in public relations—a job she loved and invested herself in completely. Both parents worked hard and did well.

The kids all did very well in school; this was, at least in part, because the parents were high achievers and had very high expectations of their kids. They were a church-going family, and the church they attended had many such high-achieving families. Church teaching also added to those expectations of high achievement and good, upright, solidly moral behavior.

If you had asked Thomas, he would have said, "We're a great family; our parents expect great things of us and that keeps us working hard; and, you know, I expect great things of myself." He probably would have agreed that the family was pretty reserved emotionally—not a lot of warmth or hugs or intense expressions of emotion of any kind. "Get to work; do your duty; we expect the very best from you—no excuses" was the unwritten rule in the family.

In high school (a fine local private school) Thomas was an achiever (no surprise there); he was president of his class; he was a track star in the spring and a talented wide receiver on the football team in the fall. He consistently made the top honor roll every year—always at or near the top academically. He didn't brag, but he was quietly proud of himself; and he kind of pitied those who didn't achieve—the goof-offs—the slow ones. He said to himself, "I'm good"; and, if truth were known, in his private thoughts, what he really said was, "I'm better."

Again, it should be no surprise that his college career was no less distinguished; he was outstanding in every way—in athletics and academics and leadership roles. And, in his sophomore year, he joined the best—the most prestigious—club on campus. He certainly enjoyed the social life there, but was careful never to over indulge. He also joined and became very active in the local campus Christian community; and, guess what? He soon became the president of that group.

I don't mean to portray Thomas as a prig; he was certainly well liked and highly respected by those around him. But there was a way he had of backing away from any situation that might even appear to get out of hand. If the club party began to get rowdy, he would fade away. He was the kind of fellow who never appeared with a hair out of place. He was at a point in his life where he was feeling pretty satisfied with all his accomplishments—satisfied and proud. "I'm good," he said ("better than," he whispered to himself).

Thomas (and his family) are the kind of people we might admire and be a bit in awe of—and probably envy a little (they look so good from outside); but I'm not sure they are people we'd really feel good about getting close to—maybe a little too perfect. But Thomas seemed pretty wrapped up in his self-satisfaction, so I imagine he was oblivious to the subtle distance between him and the folks around him; I started to say, "between him and his peers," but I don't think Thomas really quite felt that he had any peers; he was just a cut above.

Joseph Conklin (Joe) was also a member of that campus club and that Campus Christian Community. Joe was a few years older than most in his class; he had come from a pretty rough background; his father was a factory worker and his mother was a housemaid. There were lots of kids in his family. His dad regularly drank too much. There was never any extra money in his household.

And there was a period in Joe's teen years when he was rebellious; he did some drugs and was engaged in some petty theft and other gang activity; his gang had gotten pretty good at extortion. It was luck as much as anything that kept him out of serious legal trouble. He had dropped out of high school for a couple of years. But at some point he came to realize that he wanted more than the kind of punk life he was living. He was able to re-enroll in a special high school where he did well enough that he got a big scholarship to the same university where Thomas was.

Joe was much more emotionally alive and fun-loving; his rebelliousness had matured into a sort of "devil-may care" attitude; he still had a reputation as a sort of "wild man" amongst his friends, which had sort of mellowed into more of a flavor of mischievousness. Sometimes still Joe would drink too much; and, at a rather wild party he and his girl, Betty, went too far (as they say) and she got pregnant.

Wild and fun loving as he was, he had also developed some sense of honor; questions of right and wrong had not particularly concerned him during his rebellious years, but he was beginning to pay attention to his conscience. He and Betty agonized about what they should do about the pregnancy, and they felt some remorse at their carelessness.

The Campus Christian Community held a retreat not too long after this. Thomas and Joe were both in attendance.

The retreat leader was a really wise old man who had lived a long and full life. He had experienced his share of painful moments and real life struggles. He had known temptation and had given in to it more than once. He had hurt people close to him, and been hurt by them. He had known disappointment and deep loss as well as great highs and exhilarating joys—a full life, in which he had come to know through his own experience of deep shame and then forgiveness and mercy.

On the second day of the retreat, he announced at lunch that he would set aside time that afternoon to meet individually with any of the participants who wished to meet with him. Thomas and Joe each made an appointment.

Though it was not intended as a formal "confession" time, when Joe met with the leader, he poured out his heart. He acknowledged that he had behaved badly in his young life—"we beat people up and we stole stuff; we bullied people; we did cocaine," he said. Then he shared his struggle about what to do about Betty's pregnancy; he was remorseful about not having taken precautions and he acknowledged that he still tended to be something of a wild man from time to time. "But", he said, "I know these things about myself; and I'm working on them; I sure hope there is mercy and forgiveness."

The leader looked lovingly on this young man: "I can assure you that mercy and forgiveness are real," he said, "and that both are yours in abundance whenever you ask."

Thomas came in to talk about his future; his father's business was prosperous and had a place for Thomas. Thomas was excited about the prospect. Thomas was proud that he had, as the saying goes, "kept his nose clean" throughout his life. He obliquely referenced Joe—but not by name—as an example of someone who wasn't so pure; he didn't exactly express contempt for Joe, but it was clear that he felt a bit superior. He told the leader, proudly, that he had always supported the Campus Christian Community, as he had his church in his youth, with his time and energy—and his money. He was proud that he tithed. Thomas was sure that he had only a bright future ahead, and that his always upright behavior was leading to that future. He was competent in every way, and he knew it. He didn't really ask the leader for anything. His whole hour was one long song of self-congratulation.

When Thomas left the room, the leader put his head in his hands and he wept. He thought about his hour with Joe; he thought to himself, "Joe knows the 'secret'—he knows he's human—he knows that he'll screw up—and he also trusts that there is love, and support, and mercy, and forgiveness for him."

So he wept for Thomas, because Thomas seemed to need no one but himself; "how desolate—how lonely," he thought. He wept, but he didn't despair, for he knew that God (or circumstances—whichever name you want to put on it)—would bring Thomas to his knees and reveal to him his need for community—and for mercy and forgiveness. He didn't despair—but he didn't rejoice either: he didn't rejoice about the suffering and the humbling that he knew Thomas would endure, but he knew that it was absolutely necessary—and unavoidable.

I'm here to tell you, Joe left that retreat justified—made right in the sight of God. Thomas was oblivious—and alone.[11]

"I need to add this," I said: "after I preached this sermon, my theological consultant raised a question; he asked, 'So—does god favor Joe or Thomas more?' Immediately I recalled the story my friend, Will Campbell—civil rights activist, Baptist preacher, gadfly—tells about his 'conversion'. He tells of his preacher friend,

---

11. 3 Pentecost, 10/27/13; reference to Luke 18: 9-14

P. D. East, who kept pressing him to define in one sentence the essence of Christianity. Finally, Will gave in and said, 'here it is: we're all bastards, but God loves us anyway.'

"Years later, when Thomas Coleman shot civil rights worker and seminarian Jonathan Daniels to death down in Lowndes County, Mississippi, Will's friend, sat with him as he agonized over that death. Then he reminded Will of that definition, and he asked, 'Was Jonathan a bastard?' Will reluctantly had to agree that, by his own definition, Jonathan was a bastard. 'Was Thomas a bastard?' East asked. Will could more easily agree to that. Then East stared directly into Campbell's face, and said, 'Which one of these two bastards do you think God loves most?'

"So my consultant did for me what P. D. East did for Will. He reminded me of my belief in the absolute universality of God's love. When Will preached some time later about the killing and Coleman's trial and acquittal, he concluded with this, 'The maddening thing is that the Mississippi jury and God rendered the same verdict—'not guilty'.

"My consultant pressed further: 'So, what's the difference between Joe and Thomas?' The best I could come up with is this: right now, Joe is happy [Greek: *makarios* = blessed = happy] and Thomas is not. Thomas *will* be happy one day, when he's humbled enough to join the human race—to experience *all the richness* of being human (with its mixture of pain and joy, of dark and light)—but right now he's alone and unhappy."

"Earlier," I recalled, "we were talking about salvation. See what you think about this as a story about salvation:

Many years ago—many, many years ago—just after I asked Helen to marry me, she told her younger sister, Ella, "Peter and I are going to get married!"

A silence ensued . . . and then Ella said, "You can't marry Peter—he likes vanilla ice cream!"

In Helen and Ella's rather salty household, there was not much, in their estimation, that could get more bland than vanilla ice cream; not much spice in vanilla—pretty plain; pretty bland.

For some reason, an old movie came to mind as I thought about today's sermon. Some of you may have seen it—the movie is *Shirley Valentine*. You might even enjoy seeing it again. As the movie begins, we see a pleasant looking woman—with a hint of the beauty that was, but which has now morphed into a sort of frumpy housewife look— we see her talking to the walls in her kitchen in Liverpool, England. It doesn't take long for us to begin to understand through these mono- logues that she is the wife—of twenty some years—of Joe, and the mother of two grown children. They all seem to take her for granted as mother and wife, though the kids have moved out and see little of her any more. Joe expects her to maintain their solid and dull routine. In another monologue she muses, "I wonder when it happened—when I lost myself and became a missing person."

A couple of other episodes at the beginning emphasize the sense Shirley has of herself as nothing of interest—as a functionary with no real self. She is aware both that she is perceived that way by others— particularly her children and her husband—and that she has come to perceive herself that way.

Then, by chance, a divorced woman friend has won a trip for two to Greece and invites Shirley to come along—Greece being a place Shirley has wanted to visit for years (she has a touristy poster of Greece tacked to her pantry door); at first, Shirley is totally resistant to the idea—what would Joe say? And who will be there to cook for him and wash his dishes and his clothes. She acknowledges to herself that she is terrified to strike out on her own. But finally—and without ever really telling Joe that she is going (she has hinted, but never straight out said so), she goes with her friend. She leaves a note taped to the poster; Joe finds the note after she's gone, when he comes home from work. You can imagine his displeasure; his routine is disrupted!

The friend takes up with a man on the plane—and leaves Shirley to fend for herself when they get to Greece. It doesn't take long for Shir- ley to begin to enjoy herself by herself; she recognizes all of a sudden that she is an expert at being alone, so she allows herself to enjoy the place and the scenery and the chance to recover—to rescue—Shirley Valentine from being wife and mother to being, once again, herself. The first evening there, she wanders into a restaurant. She asks the waiter, whom we later discover is the owner, to move a table from the restau- rant terrace down to the path and wall near the sea—something she had dreamed of doing all the years she imagined coming to Greece.

Jesus Has Left the Building

She soon has a romantic interlude—a lovely day on his boat with the owner of the restaurant. And she assures her friend, Jane, when Jane comes back from her own fling, that she is not in love with the man—she is in love with being Shirley Valentine—alive again. At one point she muses aloud, "Why get all this life, if we don't use it?" She says to Jane, "If I don't go back, who will miss me? They may miss the mothering and the housewife, but who will miss *me*?"

Well, then the two-week vacation is over; Jane and she are at the airport preparing to board the plane to return to England. At the very last minute, Shirley turns on her heel and walks away; she returns to the village.

She spots the restaurant owner before he sees her; he is making the same move on another woman that he had made on her a few days before. He sees her and is clearly embarrassed; he comes to her. She smiles happily and assures him that he has helped her to recover herself and that she is grateful to him for that.

She tells him that she wants to be a waitress in his restaurant; he is a little taken aback, but she teases him, saying, "you surely can use some help, since you are gone so much on your boat." He laughs—and hires her.

Joe calls her several times, threatening, and then begging her to return; she assures him that she is perfectly content.

The grown son finally confronts Joe as he is going on and on about how his wife should come home. The son tells him how dull he has gotten—how imprisoned in his routine—and urges him to quit begging her to come to him and suggests that he should go to her, instead.

He does. The last scene in the movie shows him, properly dressed in dark suit and tie, walking with his suitcase up the path toward where she is sitting by the sea at a little table with a glass of wine, as she had done her very first night in Greece. Joe has wired that he is coming, so she is expecting him; she sits there waiting; she sees him, but he walks right past her without recognizing her; she calls his name. He turns, and exclaims with soft surprise, "I didn't recognize you."

I'm sure that Jesus was right—at one level—when he said something about how when spice (he references salt, specifically)—when spice loses its spiciness it is worthless and must be thrown out and trampled underfoot.

But I want to say that he is wrong, too: Shirley Valentine had lost her zest—I believe each of us is born with zest. She had lost her liveliness—her spiciness. But she got it back—both through her own initiative and also with help she gratefully accepted from others along the way—she re-claimed her self. And she may even be on the way—now that Joe took the first step—to helping Joe recover his.

I think Shirley's message is more hopeful than the message that Jesus gives in this old saying about salt being worth nothing but to be trampled underfoot if it loses its saltiness. I think the truth is that saltiness may be diluted over time, but it can't be destroyed; and it can be restored. In fact, Jesus goes on to proclaim this very truth when he declares that he is not in the business of destroying anything; rather, he's in the business of restoring—of fulfilling—everything.

So maybe this homily is, in part, an early valentine to Helen—because Ella was at least partially right about me, and Helen continues to do for me what Shirley did for Joe—and what we each have the capacity to do for ourselves and for each other—i.e., put the spiciness back in the spice.

Jesus is supposed to have said one time: "I came that they may have life, and have it abundantly."

And Shirley said it this way, "Why are we given all this life, if we don't use it?"[12]

"Well!" he said, "it's cute with a good moral—except the almost unspoken endorsement of adultery/affair putting spice in life and then equating spice to Christ's reference to the lost essence of salt. I'm not so sure about Jesus accepting Shirley's behavior to restore her essence."

"Maybe," I replied, "just maybe the way salvation happens is always a surprise. Maybe Joe will be the one to say to Shirley, 'Go, and sin no more.'"

12. 5 Epiphany, 2/9/14; reference to Matt 5:13-20

Chapter 13

Community or Institution?

"So," he said, "tell me: is church community or institution?"

"Yes," I said; "and here's another story:

"Once upon a time there was small village in a large, sparsely populated region; the people in the village all got along well; whatever chores needed to be done were shared by all. Over time, of course, the population grew and the region began to be more fully populated. People still got along quite well, but they saw the need for a person to be designated as a sort of overseer—one whose job was to see to it that all the necessary chores—services—for the region were accomplished. A man named David was chosen by the people for the position; he was a man of integrity and hard work and was known and liked by all.

"For many years the system worked well, but over time, David began to expect the people to do his bidding; understandably enough, since he was the overseer, he began to be sure that he knew best how the community should be organized. He enlisted some villagers to support his views on how everything should be done; he gave each of them a position in his administration. Taxes began to be raised both to provide services and to support the people David had hired. It was a subtle and slow-developing shift in David's attitude, but in time David began to think of the population as subservient to the institution, and not the other way around. People began to say that the overseer position had 'gone to his head'.

"A young man, named Joshua, saw this shift and was perplexed by it; he began to speak up and to suggest that David had gotten the priorities reversed. 'The institution was made to support the community,' he said; 'but, David you've forgotten that—you act like the community exists to support the institution.'"

I interjected here: "That sounds a lot like what that Rabbi said one time about the Sabbath being made for man, and so on, don't you think?"

"So, what happened?" he asked. "Did David change his ways?"

"Not yet," I replied. "But the story hasn't ended; you know, community always seems to survive and even thrive—even if it has to go underground for a time. And some David's, sometimes, see that their job is to serve the people. They are content to till the soil, plant the seeds, do a little watering and fertilizing, and then to step back, so that those communities may live and grow and blossom and beautify the world.

"So, what do you think? Is it community or institution?"

He didn't have to answer.

But I felt the need to add, "You know by now that I think the Church as institution has lots of problems and has been the cause of much misery throughout its history; and you know that I think that church as community has endless possibilities for good. But I have to be really favorable, finally, toward both Church and church, because as an incarnationalist, I can't escape the truth that you can't have one without the other—the spirit of community always has to be embodied. Maybe that is only another way that what we call 'good' and what we call 'evil' dwell together in the whole mysterious order we often call 'creation'.

"Church (as institution) provides life-giving structure for some and deadens the souls—'institutionalizes'—others. Those who have worked in prisons and those who have worked with people on welfare are familiar with the term and the reality of institutionalization. An institutionalized person is so accustomed to the life in prison—to life in the welfare system—that he literally cannot imagine living any other way.

"Brooks Hatley, played by James Whitmore in the movie, *The Shawshank Redemption*, exemplifies such a prisoner; when he is finally paroled, he has no idea what to do with himself; his life patterns of thirty plus years are totally disrupted as he sits alone in a drab apartment. He commits suicide. People who come to my office on a regular basis who have been in the welfare system for two or three generations seem totally unable to imagine living any other way.

"By contrast, Andy DuFresne, played by Tim Robbins in the movie, is in the same institution, but he manages to avoid being institutionalized. Somehow he makes the system work for him, rather than him working for the system, thus illustrating that it is possible to be in the institution but not a captive to it. (Our Rabbi is said to have said something quite similar.)

"Brooks could not believe that he was free outside the institutional walls. Andy discovered that the institution provided him some necessary structure, but did not have the power to deny his freedom.

"I know that institutions are necessary and not, of themselves, good or bad. And I acknowledge that I am speaking hyperbolically in suggesting that we, my clergy colleagues and I, are always at risk for being institutionalized—that, when we allow ourselves to focus on—and worry about—numbers and covenants and structures, we are in danger of being imprisoned. The major point I wish to make is that the good news (of the freedom with which Christ has set us free) is not a possession of the institution, and that, therefore, there are countless numbers of people in all walks of life and in all states of religion and irreligion who reside outside the institution who experience—and share—this good news. So, 'seek first the kingdom of god . . .' and all that; and 'the Sabbath was made for us and not us for the Sabbath . . .' and all that; so 'why are you afraid?' and all that.

"Here's one more sermon about community/institution:

A soldier, Staff Sgt. Travis Mills, is walking around in a gym in Spalding Rehabilitation Hospital in Boston; he lost all four limbs to an improvised explosive device in Afghanistan. He is one of several amputees from Walter Reed Medical Center in Washington, D.C. He is at Spalding to provide encouragement to those who lost limbs at the marathon bombing. He says to Paul Norden (who lost a leg), "You're not a bad person. It's not because of anything you did with your life. Things just happen." We'll come back to this, directly.

But before we do, I want to tell you about Phil Jackson, considered to be one of the finest basketball coaches ever. I heard an extensive interview with him the other day on NPR; he has just written a book entitled Eleven Rings—referring to the eleven NBA championship rings he has won as a coach. It was a delightful interview with a very interesting man. In the interview we hear about Phil's "Zen" approach to basketball and how he introduces his teams to yoga and meditation.

But the thing that impressed me most in the interview—and the thing that is at the core of Jackson's thought and coaching philosophy is the notion that, though the focus by team owners and promoters is on the super stars, what wins basketball games consistently is team work. He acknowledged that teams have to have a superstar or two to win a championship in this day and age. But his philosophy is that the stars have to incorporate all of their other teammates. Jackson is very focused on trying to make everyone on the team just as important as the stars, and on each having a real role that's meaningful. It is the "non-stars" who create the team atmosphere.

One of the major problems with the church is that we have left church to the professionals—the preachers and the theologians. Our part of the collusion is that we have abdicated; their part is that they are happy to take charge. In particular the theologians, being academically inclined and, generally, brainy folks, try in the most sophisticated ways to define God—they take common, every day human experience and fancy it up. For example: today is Trinity Sunday; the so-called Church Fathers talk about the "DOCTRINE OF THE TRINITY"—you have to say it that way when you're talking about church teaching—God as three persons but one substance—and they make that into a doctrine that all have to believe. Huh? Three in one and one in three? What does that mean and what difference does it make?

Well if we pay attention to every day experience, then we understand God from the inside, because we participate in god's life—and we have no trouble at all grasping the meaning in the notion of trinity.

I mean, look at Staff Sgt. Mills and his fellow wounded soldiers, joining with the newly wounded in Boston and forming a community. Not only does Sgt. Mills make a simple and profound basic theological statement—no—that's too fancy a way to say it: what he did was to act like Jesus. He told Paul Norden some really good news, namely 1) you are not bad; 2) this is not punishment; 3) I'm here to demonstrate that there is new life after this. So not only does he offer verbal good news to Paul, more importantly, he lives it—that is, he is living proof that they are in the same community. They are one with another—they share a common experience—a common life.

Phil Jackson knows the same thing: it is not five individuals on the basketball court—it is one team: five in one and one in five: one community, united by one spirit, having one common aim.

You get my drift? God is a community. That's what trinity means— god is community. You can see god when you see Sgt. Mills and his buddies united with Paul Norden and his buddies.

I know very little about basketball, but Phil Jackson describes a moment when the Lakers won a championship with 14.2 seconds left in the game. Michael Jordan is the super star, he's in the game, he gets the ball, he passes it to his mate, who passes it to his mate, who moves in, drawing the defense in; he passes it to his mate, who sees the fifth mate open—he passes it out to him for the winning shot. Phil's philosophy is that it is really great basketball when every member of the team touches the ball. We see God when we see every member of the team touching the ball. God is community—of which you and I are a part.

So don't worry about holding fast to the "DOCTRINE OF THE TRINITY"—just understand that god is community—and because you are in community, you are in god and god is in you—no separation.

One more story: last Thursday I was back at the Volunteer Ministry Center doing my stint as the desk attendant at the Refuge. Mid-morning a pleasant young woman walks in—no appointment— needing some clothes. The lobby was fairly full, and, as often happens, the folks in that room, having often their homelessness in common, be-gin to converse with one another. I listen and almost every week learn a new thing: for example, one woman told everybody in the room about a nearby convenience store where you can get one of those free phones and 250 minutes with no hassle. I didn't know that.

Anyhow there were three people who had come in together needing help getting identification papers; they were already a little group—a man, his girlfriend and another woman friend—and were quite friendly. They struck up a conversation with this young woman. Time went by. Lunchtime at the Mission down the street was approaching. The young woman came to the desk to see how much longer it would be before one of us could interview her. Since she was staying at the Mission, I suggested that she might walk the block and a half to the mission to eat and come back to us after lunch. She said that being eight months pregnant made that hard. One young man apparently heard that, and as he left our lobby (having been interviewed), he handed her a pack of crackers. I told the three friends, as noon was approaching, that it appeared that we would not be able to see them before our lunch break; they were cheerful about that and said they'd come back after, so they left. Though it was close to the time we closed for our break, one of our volunteer counselors agreed to see the young woman. Just before we closed down for lunch the three friends came back into the lobby to ask me if we were now interviewing the young woman. Yes. "Please tell her that we've bought her a sandwich and a drink and some chips."

And, when that young woman finished and walked out the door, she and the three had a picnic on our front stoop.

That's community—that's god—that's us.

Sgt. Mills and the amputees in Boston; Phil Jackson's team; the three amigos and the young woman; they know about community so they know about god. They don't have to subscribe to the notion of god as trinity; they know it by living it.

"Aren't we blessed to be part of the community," she said.

And the answer resounds, "we are blessed, because we are in god and god is in us—community.'"[13]

13. Trinity Sunday, 5/26/13

Chapter 14

The Clergy

"ONE OF THE BIGGEST problems the Church struggles with," I said, "is the clergy."

"Why, what on earth do you mean by that?" he asked. "What would the church be without the clergy?"

"Children are wonderful," I replied. "My great niece was three or four when her mother took her to church one Sunday morning when the bishop was making his annual visitation to their church. The bishop was all dressed up in his fancy robes and his pointy hat, and he paraded down the aisle. In a child's whisper, heard by the whole congregation, she asked, 'Who's he pretending to be?'

"Actually," I went on, "it is not just the clergy; it's the congregants, too. There's collusion between the laity and the clergy. The clergy pretend to be somebody and to know something, and lay people pretend to believe them.

"But the clergy persons' part of the blame is that they usurp the role of the laity."

"What do you mean? What role is that?" he asked.

"To be the church—to trust that in being the community, ministry happens and the good news is made manifest. The clergy, instead of being content to 'coach' from the sidelines—teaching and encouraging the laity to *be* the ministers to one another (to be a community in the ways I've been describing)—the clergy take over all the roles. They do the visitations and the pastoring and the preaching and the teaching and the counseling and the marrying and the burying. Why, many of them even try to do the business administration. Then they label various little tasks, like serving at the altar or reading a lesson or fixing flowers or preparing the coffee—they label these as 'ministries' of the laity. Can you say, 'throw the dog a bone?'"

"But," he protested, "they've been to seminary to learn to do all those ministry functions you named. The lay people don't know how."

"That's just part of the collusion," I said; "and I have two responses to the laity's claim of innocence of knowledge and ability. One, to the extent that there is special expertise involved in aspects of ministry, the clergy are to blame for failing to teach and 'coach' their parishioners and for cheating them out of their rightful place and role as church; and, two, being a friend who supports and encourages others *is* ministry—a ministry that the laity already know how to do; it requires little in the way of 'special knowledge' or 'expertise'; the laity may need encouragement and coaching, but they know how to do ministry; ministry is not the exclusive work of the clergy."

"But," he said, in further protest, "when my favorite and beloved Aunt Suzy died, I expected my priest to come to comfort me."

"You've been well trained," I said (and I thought, but didn't say, "I mean, brainwashed"). Instead, I said, "What about your good friend, Ron? Wouldn't it be a comfort to you to have your long time friend be with you in your sadness?"

"Well, yes," he said; "I would expect him to be with me; and his just being there would be a real comfort to me. But there's something about the priest's presence that is different."

I took a little while to think about that.

"I suppose you are right," I said; "perhaps in times of stress each of us needs some sense that there is an authority or power outside ourselves which may come to us to comfort us. So perhaps the difference you reference is a symbolic one—the priest is a representative—a symbol —of that outside power/authority—some would call that 'god.' It occurs to me that to the extent we need that externality, that the church community—as community—is that external authority, even if it designates one to be that symbol; it could just as well be Ron, designated as 'pastoral minister,' couldn't it?"

"I guess maybe so," he said, a bit reluctantly; "but, what do you mean questioning the need for external authority?"

"Recall what I said about incarnation—and about epistemic humility: god has incarnated in you no less than in me or anyone else, so that you have within you (and around you, in the community) all the strength that you need. At the same time, since the notion of the incarnation of god's own power is a statement of what we *believe*, real humility is called for in each of us, since we're all just bumbling around doing the best we can without knowing anything for sure. I had a good therapist friend who used to describe what he did this way, 'I just listen to people and mess around in their story'; that's what ministry is all about anyhow— messing around, trusting that god incarnates in that very activity of messing. Or, as I said about preaching, humility means that we are all just muddling through as best we can, without certainty but with a certain wonder—and maybe a little hope, combined with a pinch of trust, that life triumphs.

"It really is all about trust. The churchy word for that is 'faith'—but 'trust' and 'faith' are the same thing. As 'god' trusts us, so the clergy are to trust the people or, if churchy language helps, to trust that 'god the spirit' is at work *in the people gathered in community*. Trust the people to do the work—*trust the people."* God does.

"Here's a sermon I preached recently about that:"

In addition to the Genesis text we've just heard read—one of my favorites, as you might suspect, because its author declares that it is all good—everything is good—in addition to that text is this one that a friend sent me:

"Nothing is written until you write it."

My friend found that text both hopeful and scary. It promises a clean slate—the perpetual possibility of do-over. And it requires my friend to take charge and do it. "Nothing is written until you write it."

A story one of my seminary professors told a long, long time ago still sticks with me. After Jesus has departed this earth, so the story goes, he and God and all the heavenly council are gathered; the council members are anxious. What is to happen, they wonder, to the little band of people who had been Jesus' friends. "What is your plan now, God?" they ask. "What are the people to do, now that Jesus is no longer with them?"

"I've infused each one with my very own spirit," says God. "They have everything they need. So whatever happens now is entirely up to them."

"Well, what if they get off track? Make wrong decisions? They'll get hurt and they'll hurt one another. What then?"

"Oh, for sure, all that will happen; they will get off track, they will make wrong decisions; they will hurt and get hurt. But don't worry; in time they'll find their way. I trust them. In time they'll trust me."

"Well, what if they don't find their way? Don't you have plan B?"

"Nope. No plan B. it's now all up to them. But," he added "don't forget how it all began; it's all written up in the book: I made it all and I made it all good, and nothing can change that. So, they'll just have to come around to see that—and they will, after a while; I mean, I made them good, too."

"The trick is," he continued, "in their deciding to trust me—to believe that it's all good; once they do that, they'll become a part of making it good. You see, I depend on them, too; I depend on them to complete my good work."

"Wow," they said. "That is so liberating—and so scary."

"Yes," said God, because that is what God always says: "Yes!"[14]

"And here's the follow-up, that I preached a few weeks later:

---

14. Trinity Sunday. Reference: Gen 1:1-2:4a

Last week at the beach, my children and my grandchildren took me to school. It wasn't heavy: they taught me in the most delightful way—by being themselves.

Each year for many years, our family has gathered for a week on Topsail Island, North Carolina. Sometimes it is just immediate family but more often it includes our siblings and their spouses and children and our spouse's siblings and their children—and so on.

There are four cousins—two from my son William's family and two from my daughter Kate's family, who are stair-step close—and old enough to form their own mini-community: Alex, 10; Patrick, 9; Emma, 8; and Ella, 7.

Like all communities of people, they form and re-form; they make alliances and sub-groups; and these are ever shifting. At the same time, they are learning with each other (including, of course, learning to disagree and handle disagreements and occasional disagreeableness in each other); mostly they are enjoying each other as they learn.

So, by the middle of the week together, they decided to put on a talent show. I don't know who initiated it. It is not my business to know. They are each so creative it could have been any one of them, but I'm clear that, wherever the idea began, the final product was synergistic—the whole greater than the sum of the parts.

They created posters to put up all over the living areas, advertising the event, the time and the place. They were busy bees, buzzing about. We rent both sides of a duplex, and the theater was on the other side from my immediate family, so I only got occasional reports of how they were blocking out the routines and choreographing the action. And that is as it should be; it was their business, not mine. There was lots of activity; lots of running back and forth; lots of whispers and giggles.

The time came: as announced, after dinner on our last night—Friday. Chairs were arranged, the theater area cleared, lights dimmed. All was in readiness. Programs had been handwritten—enough copies for every one. Special VIP's were noted in the program (Aunt Connally and Cousin Lillie)—it was their living area which had been co-opted. William's two oldest, Avery, college graduate, and Ellis, entering college freshman, were listed as the make-up artists. The playbill showed Patrick as the Master of Ceremonies (and technical director); he was also listed as a player, as were Alex and Emma and Ella (and Daddy, Bill).

Great Aunt Janet knits, and she had made two cute red hats with green tops—they looked like tomatoes; the lead performance featured Alex and Emma, wearing their hats and singing the words to the song they wrote and choreographed, "We are tomatoes" as they danced around the stage. It was truly hilarious.

Ella and Emma performed a delightful song and dance routine. Alex did a beautiful ballet. Patrick maneuvered the "spotlights" (two flashlights) around to illuminate the performers; and he operated the sound system.

How clever and how kind they were: both to acknowledge and appreciate what the many elders had contributed to their production.

It was fun and funny and touching and moving. And all us adults were proud. If this sounds condescending, I have not conveyed my meaning. What I mean to say is what a truly magnificent production it was. I/we could only marvel at creative genius at work. Not "aren't they cute little children?" but, "what a marvelous creation."

And here's what I learned—once again:

As in the story I told a few weeks back—about god trusting the people, being certain that they would perform well—and about god deliberately not interfering: what we were treated to was the joyous creativity of some imaginative kids unencumbered by the controlling "wisdom" of their elders.

I imagine that, like us adults, god always delights in the unbounded imagination and creativity of her children; and god knows that they can do their best work only if she stays out of the way.

God thinks we are delightful and god delights in us. And she knows that her creativity happens through the children when we, like god, trust the process and get out of the way.

So as we with them—so god with us. "You can do it; I know you can. I leave it to you; I trust you."

And the show is a delight.[15]

15. 4 Pentecost 7-6-14

Chapter 15

The Once and Future Church

"So," HE SAID, "THE Church as we know it is badly in need of revision; from your perspective, it is currently clergy dominated, governed from 'top down', disrespectful of the very people it claims to serve, bible idolizing, and self-serving. That's quite an indictment. What ought it to look like?"

"A fair enough question," I replied, happily; "but I hope that you didn't miss the abiding good news in all that we've discussed. In the very midst of the most devastating destruction and apparent evil, the animating force for good, for life, for new life springing forth from the destruction abides and will triumph—each and every time. The shorthand word for that is 'resurrection'—it is the very core of our faith. A priest and teacher named Richard Rohr points out that we are wrong to focus on what is called 'the problem of evil'; and, sad to say, many of my clergy colleagues seem to focus more on human weaknesses and frailties. I agree with Rohr's idea that we are to focus on 'the problem of good.' He is not alone is pointing out that reality starts with an original blessing and not original sin! As Genesis says five times in a row about creation, 'It was good'; and ends with 'Indeed it was very good.' This means, I think, that there is so much good that exists in spite of what appears to be evil and destruction, that we can only marvel and wonder at how that can be so—and rejoice in it and proclaim it. The 'problem of evil' is, how is it that we spend so much time focusing on 'evil?'

Here's a good news sermon I preached not too long ago (with a brief comment about our temptation to dwell on the bad):

My father-in-law—Helen's Daddy—had many talents; but one, which to this day still absolutely astounds me, was his eye for clothes. I mean, he could go into a woman's dress shop and pick out a stunning dress for his wife or one of his daughters. He could bring it home for her to try on, and the size and the style were perfect. I couldn't do that if my life depended on it. Only one time in fifty years did I actually buy an article of clothing for Helen—a skirt, in fact—and I only dared do that by asking a woman friend of ours to go to the store with me.

As I say, there's something that still impresses me about that talent. What a wonderful thought: to be so well known and so cherished by your daddy that he clothes you in such a way as to enhance your natural beauty—and that he wants to.

I'll get back to that, but first I want to tell you about a recent experience I had: we were driving somewhere, listening to the radio. The broadcast was of the King's College Choir, from Cambridge, England, presenting the traditional lessons and carols. I'm a sucker for the refined British accent, and the boys' beautiful soprano voices and their diction and precise enunciation are simply captivating.

Following a beautiful carol or two was the reading of the first lesson beautifully spoken by one of the boy sopranos in exquisite Elizabethan English. The lesson is from Genesis, in the beautiful King James Version of the Bible, recounting how Adam and Eve are hiding in the garden and are discovered by god; and how each excuses him and herself by blaming an other. For Adam, of course, it is "the woman whom thou gavest to be with me"; for Eve, it is the serpent who "beguiled me."

Then, in this sweet, innocent, soprano voice, the boy reads the awful sentence that god is then said to have pronounced on all the miscreants:

Genesis Chapter 3: verses 14–19:
[14] And the Lord God said unto the serpent:"Because thou hast done this, thou art cursed above all cattle, And above every beast of the

field; upon thy belly shalt thou go, And dust shalt thou eat All the days of thy life.

¹⁵ And I will put enmity Between thee and the woman, And between thy seed and her Seed; it shall bruise thy head, And thou shalt bruise His heel."

¹⁶ Unto the woman He said: "I will greatly multiply thy sorrow and thy conception; In sorrow thou shalt bring forth children; and thy desire shall be to thy husband, And he shall rule over thee."

¹⁷ And unto Adam He said, "Because thou hast harkened unto the voice of thy wife, and hast eaten of the tree of which I commanded thee, saying, 'Thou shalt not eat of it':"Cursed is the ground for thy sake; In sorrow shalt thou eat of it All the days of thy life.

¹⁸ Thorns also and thistles shall it bring forth to thee, And thou shalt eat the herb of the field.

¹⁹ In the sweat of thy face shalt thou eat bread Till thou return unto the ground, For out of it wast thou taken; For dust thou art, And unto dust shalt thou return."

And, still in the sweetest of voices, having just pronounced this perpetual punishment, the boy says, "Thanks be to god." I almost laughed out loud at the irony.

But you probably won't be surprised that another reaction I had was to wonder at why it is that the church has seemed historically to assert and to focus on human wickedness—on the faults and failures of humankind. Why, in the lessons and carols, begin at chapter 3 of Genesis rather than at chapter 1—wherein god delights in all creation and repeatedly pronounces it all good?

One simple explanation is that if we celebrate the coming of a savior, a natural question is "from what do we need to be saved?" and a natural answer, then, is to focus on our human wickedness.

But chapter 1 does come before chapter 3; and what are we to make of the declaration of our inherent goodness in that first chapter?

Which suggests to me that we both can—and in fact do—select which portions of the bible to attend to the most.

And I'm not alone in believing that the church has tended throughout its long history to wallow more in sin than to rejoice in the glorious goodness which from the outset is declared to be the overarching and undergirding theme of our whole human story. Nor am I alone in asserting that the church has been wrong in that tendency. Understandable as it may be—after all, wickedness does carry a certain titillating fascination for us—we are nevertheless to look for (with the promise that when we do, we shall see) the goodness that is the basic human story.

It was today's Isaiah passage that brought to my mind the remembrance of Helen's Daddy clothing his wife and daughters in beauty. Perhaps Isaiah strikes the right balance when he acknowledges some need for restoration but focuses on and exults in the fact that we are clothed in beauty. And I'm told by those who know that when the passage in Galatians speaks of father as "Abba"—that word really translates as the familial and intimate "Daddy". It is the loving Daddy who cherishes us so much that he wants to go out himself to the store to pick out the perfect dress to enhance our beauty; and so he does. And so we are—"a crown of beauty . . . a royal diadem."

Your daddy thinks you are beautiful. Who are you to argue?[16]

"So, the church of the future? First note that in all I've said, I never implied—nor do I believe—that the church, as inspired community will ever cease to exist. Nor will the good news which the inspired community embodies ever cease to exist. For that matter, I'm convinced that the institution Church in its current 'incarnation' will also continue to exist for some time to come. Many people find inspired community in Church—that's a good thing! And at least as many people find community—and experience it as inspired—in other places and other ways—and that's also a good thing!

"So, don't hear me being 'against' Church; I am, as I said earlier, for church and for Church; it is both/and. I'm reminded of that wonderful Jewish story about Max and Isaac. They come to the Rabbi's study to settle a dispute. The Rabbi's wife is also seated in the room. Max explains his complaint to the Rabbi: the story is such and so, and he has to do this and he has to do that. He gives a fine account and argues his case clearly. The Rabbi declares, 'You're right, Max.' Next, Isaac presents his side. He speaks with such passion and persuasion that the Rabbi says to him, 'You're right, Isaac.' After they leave, the Rabbi's wife is distraught and says to her husband, 'They have conflicting stories. How can you

16. 1 Christmas, 12/29/13; reference is to Isa 61:10-62:3

say that both of them are right? When one wins, the other must lose.' The Rabbi thinks long and hard and finally says to his wife, 'You know, you're right.'

"As to the future: I think and hope that priests will continue to be well educated; they will learn to be able givers of pastoral care and designers of liturgy and preachers. But—*and here's the crucial difference*—they will learn all those things only so as to remain in the background—on the sidelines—as coaches. Think of the sermon as their 'pep talk.' They will trust that 'god' is at work in the world and in the many communities that gather at work and at play; and they will offer careful and respectful supervision of the ministers of the good news as those ministers live and work and play in all those communities. They will be the servants of the ministers, never their masters; recall that bass player I told about in the blue grass band—always in the background, providing the beat, but never up front.

"I think that the clergy will actually come to see this as liberating good news as they get freed from having to be 'professional Christians'—the ones who carry the heavy burden of dependency that any hierarchical system fosters. While I may get aggravated with my clergy colleagues from time to time, I also have tremendous sympathy for them, since it seems to me that they are as imprisoned as any one else—caught in a constricting role and longing to be free.

"My vision of clergy as coaches comes from my years as a 'supervisor' certified by the Association for Clinical Pastoral Education. My task was to stay in the background while my student pastors were out in the field doing the hands on work of providing 'pastoral' care. They would bring reports of their work to me and a small group of colleagues—from whom they would get both critique and encouragement.

"Of course seminaries will have to change rather radically and focus not only on how to think theologically but also on how to offer good coaching and supervision.

"It may be that there will be fewer large congregations; it may be that many priests will need to find so-called 'secular' jobs to support themselves as they do their coaching in small congregations.

"But whatever the structure, the good news of God will never cease to be. Communities will always exist in myriad forms and places to proclaim that good news. Even though Church as we currently know it may cease to be, recall the words of Rabbi Jesus (in my paraphrase): 'Don't just say to each other, "we are safe, for we are members of the church." I tell you that means nothing; God can raise up church—community—from these very stones.' (Luke 3:8)

"And, in those occasional moments when I allow myself to doubt my own words about church as community and people as knowing *and doing* the ministry of acting out their belief in the universal and pervasive good news of love triumphant—in those moments someone will hand me, as a good clergy friend did recently, a book of 'Advent Meditations'—or something like it. The one she gave me was written, in this case, mostly by members of a Church congregation. And in reading those I am reaffirmed once again in my belief that the people are to be fully trusted—to know and to share through beautiful, simple and heart warming stories the riches of the good news; with a minimum of 'god-talk' their stories convey the love of god made manifest.

"Or, when I doubt parishioners' capacity to be pastors, one will say to me, 'I must be away from this Church next Sunday; I have to go spend time with a friend who is grieving the death of his wife.

"How can I keep from singing?"

Jesus has left the building—with all its strictures—and beckons us to come along where life in all its chaotic glory is to be experienced—and enjoyed!